Faith Seekers; Faith Finders

Pilgrims on a Journey

William H. Jones

Faith Seekers; Faith Finders

Pilgrims on a Journey

*Seek the Lord your God, and you will find him, if you search
after him with all your heart and with all your soul.* – Moses

*Ask and it shall be given you; seek and you will find; knock
and it will be opened to you. For everyone who asks,
receives, and he who seeks finds, and to him knocks it will be
opened.* – Jesus

William H. Jones

ChiRho ☧ Communications

ACKNOWLEDGMENTS

Faith Seekers; Faith Finders was born in a 13-week documentary series, encouraged and supported by the then CTV president Douglas Bassett. The outline and narrative scripts, written by me (WHJ), were enhanced in visual format by the director, Ian Murray. Participants and presenters in the ecumenical project were leaders in six different faith groups: Earl Albrecht (a Lutheran pastor); David Apperly (a Roman Catholic deacon); Harold Burgess (a minister of the United Church of Canada); Gordon Fish (a Presbyterian minister); Timothy Foley (an Anglican priest); William H. Jones (a Baptist pastor). Each of the presenters researched specialized backgrounds and presented them as part of the story-telling in TV "stand-up" form.

Their "stand-ups" do not appear as such in this book. The standups don't work in book format. Rather, I have rewritten and boxed "sidebars" on some of the topics these items formerly presented in television form.

The work and encouragement of the foregoing presenters is appreciated. It is to them that this book is dedicated. A sequel to this book will be published as *The Quest for Soul Liberty*, another 13-week CTV documentary from where *Faith Seekers; Faith Finders* has left off. David Apperly and Harold Burgess are gone from this life and now enjoy more fully the presence of God. WHJ

TABLE OF CONTENTS

Choosing Saul's Successor
The Cave of Adullam
Abigail and David's Wives
David and the Jebusites
The Great Temple
Solomon's Mines
The Pillars of Solomon

Role of the Prophets
Samuel: Prophet of Renewal
Some Minor Prophets
Isaiah: The Making of a Prophet
Ezekiel: Priest, Prophet, Preacher
Haggai: Temple Builder
Malachi: Messenger to the Bored
Zechariah

Sebaste / Samaria
Who Are the Samaritans?
Sennacherib
Changes During Exile
Nehemiah
Ezra
What is a Synagogue?

Antiochus Epiphantes
The Maccabee Family

The Herods
The Pharisees
The Sadducees
Herodians
Essenes

Jesus, the Christ
Rahab: Jesus' Ancestry
Nabateans
What is a Bar Mitzvah?
John the Baptist
Purification Rituals
Jesus Begins his Ministry
Jesus, the Healer
The Beatitudes

Belittled Bethlehem
Neglected Nazareth
Commercial Capernaum
Blessed Bethany
Zion's Slums
Jeweled Jerusalem

The Transfiguration
Jesus Sets his Face to Enter Jerusalem
Jesus Weeps over Jerusalem
The Last Supper

INTRODUCTION

How do you condense 2,000 years of history from Abraham to Jesus in less that 200 pages? The answer is you can't.

This book, then, simply highlights some of the people and events in that time period. The Bible does not always tell us some of the historical factors that surround the biblical characters. So this book highlights some of them, such as the Maccabees and Antiochus Epiphanes – and many more.

The reader is encouraged to delve more deeply into some of the backgrounds of this time period.

But the most important parts of this book tell of the biblical events. They draw us closer to the work of God through his people and his Son.

CHAPTER 1

AN IMPRESSIVE FAITH JOURNEY

The procession started with Abram. He and his father moved from Ur of the Chaldees to Haran in step one of a great migration. In step two, Abram trekked from Haran, in today's Turkey, to a land of promise. In the midst of moon worshippers, did Abram start to get a sense of what is holy?

His was a pilgrimage as surely as anyone's journey to the holy land. Yes, the soil itself was sacred, set apart, prepared for those who wanted to know, feel, search for and obey God. Abraham's people had a sense of "serving the land." It was not to be used or abused; soil and stones were sacred trusts.

Stones and soil were holy on two counts. One reason for their sacred nature was that God had promised this land to Abram. That made it holy to the patriarch, at least, and therefore to his descendants. Secondly, the land was holy because it provided food to eat and nourished the herds and flocks which grazed its fringes.

It was holy to the point that every meal eaten was preceded by the recognition that God provided the land to give food. In a sense, Abram and his descendants "served" the land. When they broke bread and drank wine, or tarried over a meal, they remembered who it was who was the Provider. "Blessed are you, King of the universe," went the prayer, "for you have brought forth food from the earth."

**"Abraham was the father of Isaac,
Isaac the father of Jacob
Jacob the father of . . ."**

Three of the world's greatest religious families –
Christianity, Judaism and Islam – draw from the same
biblical wells.

**"... the father of Boaz, whose mother was Rahab,
Boaz the father of Obed, whose mother was Ruth ..."**

Faith Seekers; Faith Finders follows a family
lineage – beginning 4,000 years ago – from Abraham to
Jesus and recounts their discoveries of the spiritual heritage
which has supported modern peoples' struggle to know God.

**"... the father of Jesse
and Jesse the father of King David.
David was the father of Solomon, whose mother had been
Uriah's wife,
Solomon the father of ..."**

Throughout this book we will discover the
progressive nature of faith and its revelations. God seemed
to disclose himself in different ways to different people.
Usually the revelations were made to individuals of special
character. Sometimes the faithful took four steps forward and
three back. They were often disobedient and flawed in
character. Yet God never gave up on them, constantly telling
those who would listen that he was prepared to meet any
who would come to him in a trust relationship and in
commitment.

Geography and history, mores and culture are all
components of the biblical picture in which human
spirituality and divine faith are forever intermixed. In this
book we shall examine the soil and the stones of the land and
the beliefs and experiences of those from whose spiritual

roots we have evolved.

**". . . the father of Jacob,
and Jacob the father of Joseph, the husband of Mary, of whom was born Jesus, who is called Christ."**

Abram's was a faith journey of impressive dimensions. He was leaving what was familiar for what was unknown. Abram had come to trust the God he scarcely knew. Yet his new God was not only the God of promise, but his friend.

THE NOMADIC LIFE

Nomads seldom settle in one place. They prefer to wander freely, have no permanent residence and, as itinerants, worry about precious few possessions. Nomads employ unspoken rules. No public laws existed. The rule of lex talionis, "an eye for an eye and a tooth for a tooth" was clearly underlined, even if done so silently. Mutuality of basic existence led to their understanding involving grazing rights, certainly access to water. All issues focussed on mutual survival. Nomadic people found their identity in the tribe, not in the nation. They still do.

Tribal nomadic societies, of which the bedouin are one, are headed by a [shaykh] "sheikh," sometimes elected, but usually is an elder who, as a natural leader, seems to enjoy an authority as first among peers. Such leadership was undergirded by advisors in a council of family heads. While this reflects a patriarchal system, and women existed to serve the men, some wives exerted quiet and manipulative pressures to get their own ways. "Sheikh" Abram, on the other hand, regarded his wife Sarai as more than a servant.

Somehow the bedouin life has survived to this day. Many of them would not see asphalt highways and street lights as progress. They still prefer the traditions of the many millennia – camels dressed up for a family wedding, cooking pots of an old design, with meals cooked over traditional campfires.

These nomads moved from one grazing ground to new pasture often without regard for their exploiting the land their flocks and herds had exhausted. The people of the Hebrews later spoke of "serving the land" – a sense of stewardship in their admiration for the soil which was God's gift to them.

Many of Abram's other bedouin fellow travellers misused

the soil, spending it poorly, creating deserts by their callous overuse of grazing areas.

In Abram's journeys, the Bible notes that he sometimes settled in areas for a surprisingly lengthy sojourn. We note that Abram stayed for a while at Shechem, Beth-el and Hebron and that Isaac settled at Gerar. Their travels generally followed the ridges of the land, leaving the valleys for cultivation.

And so, from father to son, it was told around bedouin campfires and remembered today nearly four millennia later, that Abram was the friend of God.

Abram's father was Terah the Sheik, Terah, the former moon-worshipper, who departed Ur with his wives, his children, his servants, flocks and herds. Ur, a great city of the ancient world, lay nearby the Euphrates River, southeast of Babylon. In its Third Dynasty, 200 years before Abram, the city boasted wide influence over other Mesopotamian cities, and was renowned for its advances in lawgiving, and its pyramid-like Ziggurat which served as a towering temple to the moon god.

Perhaps Terah and Abram left Ur as that Mesopotamian city was in its descendancy. Yet they also were drawn westward toward Haran, in what today is Eastern Turkey, drawn by some spiritual insight of a deity who was revealing to him and their family that the moon did not rule the universe, but only the one universal, unseen God.

Terah died in Haran, but at age 75, his son Abram, later to be known as Abraham, was also drawn by the one who revealed himself as the true and only God. Abram was not driven, but drawn, toward a destiny and destination not quite known to him, not westward but southward from Haran to the land of Canaan.

True, the nomad life was one continual faith journey. The richer the sheik, the more faith was required to find soil and fodder for grazing animals. Every day was a new day for the nomadic families, searching for sustenance and protecting good grazing ground from other nomads.

When a sheik had found a place to stay he obeyed the instinctive rituals of pitching camp. Every family member had an assignment. Every servant knew just what to do. The goats, sheep and cattle willingly obeyed the call to pasture and grazed in relative comfort. Among the rituals was the appropriate obeisance to the deity who was the family's protector and sustainer.

So when Abram's caravan settled temporarily at Shechem in central Canaan, the patriarch immediately built an altar to the LORD – his friend in faith.

The migrant Abram merely paused at Shechem in Samaria. Shechem means "shoulder," so named, perhaps, because it was on the shoulder of the road which coursed between Mount Gerezim on one side and Mount Ebal on the other. When Abram arrived there, *en route* from Haran, God, not yet known as YAHWEH, revealed himself to Abram. So Abram set up an altar (Genesis 12:7) at Shechem where he offered sacrifice to the God who led him to that place and promised this territory to him, together with his offspring -- probably including his nephew, Lot.

The altar sacrifice had two purposes. The spiritual significance of it is apparent. Here, in this act of sacrifice, Abram demonstrated unequivocally that he sought communion with his God. Moreover, he was a thankful person who did what was appropriate to express his gratitude for God's mercy. It was a holy "place," for here God provided him with a special revelation of the future.

But this act of devotion was more than a spiritual endeavour. It was a political move as well. Locals observing the nomad Abram and his company at worship would note that Abram was a powerful man, considering his movable wealth of cattle, sheep, goats, servants and family.

More important, observers would see that Abram probably worshiped a most powerful God. In other words, the altar worship by Abram was a strong signal to everyone around, that he was not alone; he was indeed led and protected by an unusual, unseen and very secure deity. Let anyone worry who would attack Abram.

Abram, nomad that he continued to be, found it necessary to take his caravan toward Egypt during one intense period of drought and famine in Canaan. The man of faith proved to be surprisingly insecure as he ventured into the territory of Philistia at Gerar. In such a setting, he could see that some powerful potentate might kill him just in order to add his attractive wife Sarai to his harem. Abram told Sarai to say that she was his sister, should anyone inquire.

The very thing happened. King Abimelech's servants suggested to him that indeed Sarai should be added to his household. As compensation, a kind of dowry, the king rewarded Abram with ample sheep, cattle, donkeys, camels and slaves, both male and female.

But when Abimelech's household became ill, the king of Gerar concluded that he had offended Abram's deity. He returned Sarai to Abram, and told them to leave his territory. Once more, Abram turned his face in the direction of Canaan to the fields and pastures of Beth-el, where his animals had grazed earlier.

THE BUILDING OF ALTARS

Altars introduce themselves early in the Bible. We learn about a dispute between Cain and Abel who fought about the worth of their sacrifices. An altar was where a gift could be given to God. Usually it comprised a pile of rough stones, often with corners marked by higher ridges. Altars occasionally took the form of a stone slab or even sod.

As people moved their worship into temples, the altars became more stereotyped and elaborate. In all ancient regions, the altar became a key symbol of genuine worship, particularly of devotion, honour and commitment. An animal or bird was often offered as a gift to God, and this shedding of blood, represented both loyalty to God and God's willing forgiveness for any offence which may have been committed against him.

There is a sidebar to this act of devotion. When Abram moved into his promised land, initially he built two altars. One was at Shechem, the other at Beth-el. Shechem was already a religious centre for the Canaanites. It was marked by a grove of oak trees. Thus, Abram's altar was first an act of devotion, and secondly a stake in territorial rights.

The altar was Abram's warning to the Canaanites that his God was now the deity of this location. "Keep your distance," he was tacitly saying, "Give me respect, because my God has now given it to me."

Nomads tended to do that because while a usurper might attack another band of nomads, he could not easily measure the power of the nomad's deities. The act of worship was therefore more than an appeasement to one's god; it was also a signal to all who watched that "My God will protect me. If you fight me, you will also have to fight my God."

LOT'S CHOICES

*Abram, because he had deceived the Pharaoh, was invited
to leave Egypt (Gen. 13). The famine in Canaan was over.
Lot and Abram argued about the scarce pasture land and
agreed to separate. Lot chose the fertile Jordan Valley, and
settled close to the notorious city of Sodom. Later,
Lot and the Sodom's king, along with all of Lot's family,
flocks and herds, were kidnapped in a border-raid. Lot
offered no resistance. Abram heard of the disaster,
organized some 314 his own men, pursuing the raiders and
defeating them. Abram's army freed Sodom's king and Lot
and retrieved all his lost possessions. Lot chose to live within
Sodom, even amid Sodom's homosexual practices.*

*Angelic messengers in the guise of ordinary men,
visited Abram, telling them God's intentions to destroy
Sodom. Abram priested with them for the city's future. The
heavenly messengers made their way to Sodom and Lot's
house.*

*Learning of the strangers' arrival to their city certain
"lewd fellows of the baser sort" (to quote Acts written
centuries later) besieged Lot's house demanding that the
strangers be surrendered to them for their carnal purposes.
Instead, Lot offered his virgin daughters to appease the
crowd. Angelic visitors took command, drew Lot back into
the house, struck the attackers blind.*

*They urged Lot and his family to flee the city, for God
was displeased with its evil ways. In the morning the family
did flee, but Lot's wife, looking back, became a pillar of salt.
This story was repeated around the campfires of God's
Chosen People, generation after generation; and in due time
was incorporated into the record of Genesis.*

Abram's nephew Lot and his family may also have journeyed to Egypt with Abram, but once back, their servants began their bickering again. Disputes arose between the servants of Abram and those of Lot over the rights to specific grazing areas and wells.

Abram and Lot did not spat with each other; indeed the opposite is true. Abram had high regard for Lot, and later was to avenge his kidnapping.

So the patriarch Abram offered Lot his choice of pasture and wells, and where his clan would settle. Less generous than Abram, Lot opted for the more fertile soil in the Dead Sea valley near Jericho.

The notorious cities of Sodom and Gomorrah were utterly destroyed. To this day their ruins have neither been fully authenticated nor identified. Scholars generally believe that the ruins may be buried beneath the salt deposits of the Dead Sea.

The Dead Sea is now a source for a generous supply of minerals. It has also grown to be a vacation spot for Jerusalemites, and has become famous for its health spas which offer cures or remissions of various illnesses and health conditions such as psoriasis.

The Jerusalem which modern vacationers may have left for a time at the Dead Sea resorts remains a centre of faith for many religions, especially Christianity, Judaism and Islam. Faith sometimes reflects territory and mores, and when these are threatened, conflict quickly ensues. The pattern of instant conflict has repeated itself over many centuries.

MELCHIZEDEK: PROTOTYPE PRIEST

Abram became a powerful sheik who ranged in the Negev desert. His servants formed an army strong enough to recapture his nephew Lot who, with his family, herds and flocks, had been abducted to Damascus.

En route home, Abram travelled by Salem – what later would be called Jerusalem – and met Melchizedek, Salem's king and priest. His name means "The King is Righteous." This mysterious figure is described as a "priest of the Most High God, El Elyon." They held a symbolic communion together and made a covenant.

In the biblical book of Hebrews, Melchizedek is described as a person without father, mother or genealogy. Thus Christ is compared to the ancient priest / king – "after the order of Melchizedek that unlike the priest Aaron, had no father or mother . . . Christ also had no such genealogy and has neither the beginning of days nor the end of life."

Yet Jerusalem, (in Hebrew, Yer-u-shal-eye-im) means "dwelling of peace" – so named by King David. Jerusalem's ancient name was Salem from the Semitic word which gives us "shalom." Four thousand years ago, Abram and his army of 314 passed by this area, and encamped near the city state of Salem. This city with its reputation for a peaceful co-existence with its neighbours may have anxiously pondered the intentions of Abram and his imposing army.

For sure, Abram was a saint with clay feet, generous towards Lot, unassuming toward God, while refusing to get rich by claiming loot from his raid on

ABRAM MOVES ON

This encounter was between righteous men with kindred minds. In a world where the populace worshipped many gods, here were two great men of faith in communion with each other and with the one God in whom each of them believed. Abram knew his God by a different name, not yet as YAHWEH. Melchizedek called his God El Elyon. But they were one and the same.

Abram saw the divine presence in Melchizedek. Abram accepted the priest's hospitality of bread and wine, and held a private "holy communion" with him on the edge of Jerusalem.

In their covenant, Melchizedek blessed Abram and praised God for Abram's military successes. Abram answered the blessing with a tithe of everything he had captured from the Syrian thieves.

As Abram concluded his covenant visit with the priest and king of Salem, the patriarch divided the remaining spoils of his conquest with his supporting troops. He kept nothing for himself. He had but one objective and it was not to enrich himself, but to liberate Lot and company.

the kidnappers of Lot. However, Abram was capable of self-interest, fear, deceit and duplicity.

Yet we see him also as a man who earnestly priested – begged, pleaded and bargained with his friend God – on behalf of the wicked leaders of Sodom. It is instructive that he cared so deeply about others, even those who were so injurious to his nephew Lot and his family. This giant man of faith began to show that love extends even to one's enemies!

Abram resettled in two main areas of Canaan, in Be'ersheba and Hebron. From Mamre, in the outskirts of Hebron, Abram learned that Sarai would become a mother to his promised son.

At Mamre, Abram's name was changed by God to Abraham. Abram meant "exalted father," and Abraham meant "father of many" – an indication of his generations yet to come. God solemnly promised his friend that he would be the "father of many nations."

Abraham seemed to prefer Be'ersheba as his final home, and except for his purchase of a family burial site near Hebron for his wife, appeared to own no land. Yet the land was his and his children's by mutual consent with the other bedouin leaders and by commission of the LORD.

In answering Abraham's prayers, God promised him

BE'ERSHEBA

Be'ersheba became the southern boundary of The Promised Land. The northern limit was Dan. Be'ersheba became the first main temporary residence of Abraham, and Isaac, his son. The patriarch stopped here because it had a well – and still has one.

God met both father and son in this place and spoke to them, thereby increasing its spiritual significance. God made promises to them both and assured his protection as they travelled.

Both built altars to acknowledge that God was in this semi-desert place.

Today, it sports a weekly market for bedouin who gather to buy and sell livestock.

---

a son. When Sarah was past her child-bearing years, the blessed event occurred. She conceived. Their son Isaac commenced the lineage which God promised to his obedient believer and trusted friend, Abraham.

When Abraham had buried his wife, there seemed only one last challenge to him. That was to find a wife for his son Isaac. It was important to find the right wife for him, because of the sacred promise which God had made to Abraham about him being the father of many nations. As we shall see in the next chapter, that also was fulfilled for Abraham in God's unique way.

CHAPTER 2

A SUCCESSION OF PATRIARCHS

In the previous chapter we saw how a man named Abram (Abraham) moved from Ur of the Chaldeans into the land of Canaan. He moved even farther spiritually, from mingling with moon-worshippers in Ur and Haran to embracing the concept that there was but one true God, and to learn he could trust that God as his friend.

Almost 4,000 years ago, Abraham lived and died, and was buried with his wife, Sarah, in the Cave of Machpelah, a plot of ground he bought as the family burial site. His life is honoured today also by Jews and Muslims because they see him as the progenitor of their faith. They celebrate the Cave by a mosque which covers the traditional burial site of that ancient patriarch and his family.

Before Abraham died, however, he assured that his seed would survive by having his faithful servant swear a most sacred oath, that he would help find a bride for his precious son, his miracle-given grown son, Isaac.

The nomadic civilization in which Isaac lived had no charter of rights but significant silent and spoken responsibilities. Families found security within the mores and conditions of clan life. The dominant figure was the father, and sons had priority of place over daughters.

Yet women too had a matriarchal presence, with unseen influence and power, often swaying the decisions of the patriarch himself. As someone wryly stated, "The head may rule the house but the neck turns the head." Deals and contracts had a sacred aspect to them and covenantal relationships were only broken upon pain of social ostricization or on occasion, significant and repetitious feuds

ISAAC TAKES A WIFE!

Abraham was consciously aware that God had specifically honoured him both as a person and for a duty. God commanded him tell the people of the world about God, his name and his sovereignty. All the world, through this Patriarch would learn of and be blessed by God's love and character.

Abraham knew his son Isaac needed a wife to continue this special blessing and responsibility. Since all ancient marriages were arranged – usually convenient contracts for political and social welfare of the parents – Abraham resolved that Isaac must not intermarry a Canaanite woman whose upbringing included pagan deities and pagan ideals.

The patriarch sent a trusted servant to find such a wife. The servant set out with a prayer on his lips, that the LORD would provide a helpmate for Isaac.

When a woman named Rebekah came to the oasis well where the servant had paused with his camels, God answered the prayer. With typical bedouin courtesy, Rebekah offered water for the camels. After introductions, Rebekah's brother, Laban, showed interest in the marriage proposition, and Rebekah freely consented to the marriage arrangements. Rebekah's father was Bethuel, but Laban did the talking and negotiating.

Upon arriving in Isaac's camp. Rebekah was flustered when she met her husband-to-be. The Bible says "she fell off her camel." While she didn't get a second chance to make a first impression, Isaac was chivalrous. The Bible reads, "he brought her into the tent of his mother Sarah and he married Rebekah. So she became his wife, and he loved her; and Isaac was comforted."

RIGHTS OF THE FIRST BORN

Even today, royalty chooses the firstborn, usually a male, to inherit the monarch's throne. In earlier times it was agreed that the firstborn should inherit. That preserved peace within the family and the tribe. It prevented continuing strife for power and possession. Ancients generally believed that the firstborn male belonged to the god or gods who gave life. Either he must be offered as a sacrifice, or preferably be redeemed by proper payment. So the first born male had an aura of holiness. He was a proof of his father's virility.

Societies generally recognized that within the family or the clan, the first-born son had more status. He had responsibility, authority and even a sense of sanctity as his birthright. He would usually succeed to his father's position and the majority of his father's possessions.

Jacob, the younger of Isaac's twins, conspired to change this law of succession. Jacob noted that his slightly older twin brother, Esau, was more interested in food than in family futures, so in a swap of food for birthright, Jacob demanded surrender of his valuable birthright. Esau, feeling famished to death, agreed and ate.

Their father Isaac grew old and blind and near to death. Jacob, with the connivance of Rebekah, his mother, stole the commission and blessing belonging to the older son. With his hands on Jacob's head, the deceived father prayed: "God give thee the dew of heaven and the fatness of the earth and plenty of corn and wine. Let nations serve thee, and nations bow down to thee. Be lord over thy brethren, and blessed be he that blesseth thee." The blessing his, Jacob fled his brother's wrath. But the birthright was his!

Isaac and Rebekah's firstborn were twins – two boys, Jacob and Esau, or to put them in the right order of birth, Esau and Jacob. And when a father has a bent towards the more virile of the two, and the mother an affection more toward the gentler twin, is not trouble in the offing?

Among the accepted norms of nomadic society were socially-held beliefs that the firstborn son was a special divine gift, an honour from God, and a signal of the deity's pleasure. Nomadic life translated into continual mobility for every family. When the rains did not come to Isaac's Canaan – and the grasses were parched and sere – famine spread over the area of Canaan where Isaac and Rebekah kept their possessions.

Warned by God not to travel to Egypt as did Isaac's father Abraham in an earlier famine, and encouraged by God to keep faith with him and obey his directions, Isaac limited his sojourn to find grasslands to the coastal areas inhabited by the Philistines.

Again history repeated itself. This time it was Isaac, fearing for his life among strangers, who was prepared to pass off his beautiful and fetching Rebekah as his sister, so that should the king of the Philistines want her for his harem, he would not kill Isaac to take her.

But the Philistine king, Abimelech, discovered that Rebekah was really Isaac's wife – because he saw Isaac caressing her – and so he confronted Isaac with the discovery. And to Abimelech's credit, he made a covenant to protect the patriarch, Isaac.

Eventually, when Isaac's wealth grew to great proportions, and the Philistines grew uneasy with such a powerful bedouin in their midst, Abimelech suggested – emphatically! – that Isaac leave lest there be fighting among his people.

COVENANTAL RELATIONSHIPS

Covenants were pivotal to religious and social life in the biblical world. The dictionary defines "covenant" as a "binding agreement." It suggests that two parties found a common ground which was mutually acceptable to them. Covenants are not necessarily only biblical – ancient systems and societies all used covenants. No covenants were made flippantly. All covenants were serious business.

Noah and Abraham each covenanted with God. When Moses gathered the newly freed Israelites in Sinai's wilderness, he revealed God's covenant with the people. Years later, King Josiah became aware that Israel's covenant with God had been dishonoured, so the king renewed the pledge once more, vowing "with all his heart and with all his soul" to rid the nation of its idolatry and alien deities.

The "Book of the Covenant" is found in the mid chapters of Exodus and was restated in the book of Deuteronomy, the mishnei ha-torah, or the "copy of the law." This Book of the Covenant set forth the terms by which Isaac's God would be related to by the Israelite people. God would keep his promise if the nation honoured its pledge.

Covenantal society required a form of law which would be honoured, understood, respected and obeyed by both covenanting parties. These agreements were not necessarily between equals, although in some instances of marriages or business transactions they may have been. In the covenant between Isaac's God and the people, the agreement was not between equals. Covenants defined justice and set community standards. These included a requirement for every Israelite to present himself, that is, to offer a sacrifice before the LORD known as YAHWEH, God's understood, unspoken personal name. This

Such agreements and covenants made between people like Isaac and Abimelech were important concepts for successful clan continuity and tribal interactions.

While preservation of the clan was an imperative of bedouin life, the necessity of family solidarity was often interrupted by rebellious children competing for tribal leadership. Esau, lacking the birthright he traded to his brother, saw little reason to continue in his family's tradition.

The Bible tells that there was in-law trouble between Isaac and Rebekah and Esau's chosen wives. Esau had chosen his marriage partners from among the Canaanite women, that is, from among those who neither acknowledged nor obeyed the God of Abraham, Isaac and Jacob.

Referring to the daughters-in law, the Bible puts it, "They made life bitter for Isaac and Rebekah." Was it because Isaac still believed he would pass along the birthright to Esau? Or, possibly the enmity existed because Esau refused the spiritual inheritance which was his on any account.

Spiritual dimensions were also wrapped up in the covenantal communities. Now Abraham and Isaac had new understandings of the one true God, who is personal, yet creator of the heavens and the earth.

He is one who reveals himself to humans. We see evidence of that in the family feud between Jacob and the scheming scamp Laban.

Obviously Rachel felt more secure with the traditional household fertility gods and lacked the spiritual insight that Jacob was gradually gaining.

When the Bible relates its stories of the patriarchs, tales likely told around the campfires of bedouins, year after year, generation after generation, it reveals warming tributes to some characteristics of Jacob, even as it reveals his darker personality. We see Jacob yearning for a reconciliation with his brother Esau. To be sure, there was a practical aspect of such reconciliation.

In the mideastern world of waterless wastes, it was essential to have an alliance with someone who would permit another to use his wells.

HOUSEHOLD GODS

Ancients kept household gods. Rachel stole Laban's household deities when she married Jacob. He and his wives left Laban's oasis and set out on their own. Unknown to Jacob, Rachel had placed the terephim in her saddle bags. Laban found them missing, and in hot pursuit, overtook Jacob's group en route to Canaan.

Rachel protested she had not taken these gods and invited Laban to search, except that she was ritually unclean because of her time of estrus. Had Laban touched the saddle, with Rachel sitting on it, Laban would have been ritually unclean too, and would have needed to go through all the ritual cleansing that was required of "uncleanness."

Maybe the household gods needed cleansing too, or was the thought that they had power over such things?

JACOB AND GOD'S LADDER

On one of his journeys, Jacob headed out from Be'ersheba to far-off Haran. On the way he stopped at a sheltered place which seemed suitable for overnight. Travelling lightly, he lacked the customary pallet for sleeping. For a pillow he chose a flat stone.

Soon Jacob was asleep and began to dream. In his vision he saw a ladder reaching from earth to sky and on the ladder were God's messengers climbing and descending as they performed their duties in keeping with God's orders. Above the ladder stood the LORD himself, and from his heavenly abode the LORD spoke to Jacob revealing himself by name: "I am the LORD, the God of your father Abraham and the God of Isaac. I will give you and your descendants the land on which you will be lying . . . I will watch over you wherever you go, and I will bring you back to this land. I will not leave you until I have done what I have promised you."

Immediately upon awakening, Jacob sensed the awesomeness of the very place he had been resting. He believed he had stumbled onto the special, sacred site where God revealed his will to humankind, where angels descended from heaven and entered the earth or ascended from the earth to enter heaven.

This was a current belief of many religions during Jacob's time, that there were special openings into the heavens. If one ventured onto such a celestial gateway, one could be condemned should he desecrate it. The appropriate response of such an invasion should be reverence and worship. The Bible tells us that Jacob took his pillow stone, set it up as an altar to the LORD and poured oil on it as an appropriate libation.

> *The Hebrew word bayith means, "where you spend the night," In other words, "house." So Jacob called this place "Beth-el," the "house of God." Said Jacob in this now-sacred place, "This is none other than the house of God; this is the gate of heaven."*

Apparently Jacob earnestly wanted to put behind him the life-long feud which had been running with his twin and competitor, Esau. Jacob spent a long night praying to God to ease the tension between them to heal the wounds of bitterness, and to resolve the enmity which made them competitors and rivals.

That set the stage for a remarkable faith experience for Jacob. He now knew the One who made the heavens and the earth, one who is personal, intimate, and reveals himself to humans.

The revelation of God came by stages, a progressive revealing of who God was and what he was like. At times the insights of deity gained by Abraham, were lost by Isaac and by Jacob. Yet each grew spiritually, while remaining human with natural inclinations. Each was on the growing edge of spirituality, in spite of their continuing spiritual failures.

As Jacob, now called Israel, grew older and found peace with his brother Esau, he also found renewal of faith and purpose with his God. We find him rebuilding and rededicating altars – at Shechem, where his grandfather Abraham first built an altar to God, and at Beth-el, where he had the vision of the stairway to heaven.

While Abraham brought the divine revelation to his people, that there was but one God, creator of the heavens and the earth, and that God was personal and commissioned those who believed on him to tell his name and character to

JACOB BECOMES ISRAEL

Jacob learned to wrestle with God. After the matter was settled he learned that God really wins every time but sometimes lets us think the victory is ours. The wrestling began with a dream where the patriarch climbed into the heavens and was rewarded with insights he had not previously understood.

What he learned was that he had been too deceitful for God's liking, especially since the LORD intended to use Jacob for divine purposes – to lead his offspring into a new relationship with the Almighty.

When Jacob acknowledged his deceit and submitted to God, the LORD changed the Patriarch's name from Jacob (Deceiver) to Israel (Prince). They made a pact, a covenant together, Prince and God, and to remember that pledge, God gave a distinct limp to Israel.

all the peoples, it was Jacob who gave his name to the land and to the people. Israel! "You have struggled with God and overcome!"

But as we shall see in the next chapter, the people who "contended with God and won," soon would have to contend with the Egyptians and win.

CHAPTER 3

FINDING BREAD IN STRANGE PLACES

In the previous chapter, we noted how Isaac and his son Jacob began to take seriously the notion that they had a unique and privileged relationship with God. Jacob's name was changed by God, from Jacob, which meant "supplanter,"or "cheat," to Israel, which meant "overcomer," "Prince," or "power of God." If people live up to the name that is given to them, Jacob, now renamed Israel, learned to do just that, to overcome! As God gave Israel his new name, he also gave him a new ideal.

Israel's grandfather, Abraham, sensed that God had chosen his family to convey the divine revelation to mankind. The revelation disclosed that God was not to be found in the created order and worshipped as sun or moon, but that he, God, created all things, and wanted a relationship with all of creation, especially a personal involvement with humankind. Faith seekers can become faith finders.

When Isaac died, Jacob grew spiritually, and in his latter days, renewed his affection for God. Renamed Israel – the name means, in part, "He contended with God and men and won," Israel accepted his patriarchal destiny to convey the divine revelation to his offspring and family – the "children of Israel."

Jacob married twice, once out of duty and once out of love. Jacob himself waxed cunning and political but he met his match among one of his own family members – the manipulator Laban.

Jacob wanted to marry Rachel because she was more beautiful. But Laban intended to have Jacob marry Leah, because she was the eldest daughter. On the day of the

JACOB'S TWO FAMILIES

Jacob had two wives – and two families. They were two very different families, one from the preferred wife of Jacob, and the other one he was pressured to wed. Naturally, the children of the preferred wife (Rachel) became the preferred children. Such dysfunction begets trouble.

Each of Jacob's offspring gave their names to the tribal entities of the Israelite people. A half-millennium later, when the conquered territory of Canaan became Israel, the territories borrowed the names of Jacob's descendants. There was no named tribe of Joseph, however.

wedding Jacob married a veiled bride – and there the intrigue began. Despite the nomadic tradition of the eldest son's birthright, it may have been natural for Jacob to dote more on Rachel's offspring than on Leah's.

That was the way it turned out. To Rachel were born Joseph and Benjamin. Sadly, when Benjamin was born at Bethlehem, Rachel died during the childbirth. As a result, Joseph and Benjamin became the more precious to their father Jacob. This added fatherly affection, together with the diminution of traditional rights of the eldest, became a cause of much jealousy among Jacob's other family.

It seems that Joseph also lorded his status over his elder brothers. Joseph was also precocious, and received revelations in the form of dreams. Since sleep fascinated ancient man, dreams were given the status of reality and of divine prophecy. In his dreams, young Joseph often told of situations in which his brothers were required to give their obeisance to him.

The irritations could no longer be repressed. One day the brothers, while pasturing their herds at Dothan far from Jacob, conspired to kill 17-year-old Joseph. They relented, only to sell him to some Ishmaelite spice tradesmen – the Bible says they were "laden with balm and myrrh" – on their way from the east side of the Jordan River, past Dothan to trading centres in Egypt. The brothers took the multi-coloured coat of Joseph, smeared it with blood and reported to their ageing but heavy-hearted father, Jacob, that Joseph had been torn to pieces by some ferocious animal.

Meanwhile, in the Nile Delta, Joseph began his own destined adventure, moving from being a slave to Potiphar, to becoming one of Pharaoh's officials. His moral correctness, of spurning the advances of Potiphar's wife, landed him in prison – and for two years, oblivion.

So the brash, opinionated, 17-year-old braggart Joseph had grown up. Moreover, he matured to exhibit both keen foresight and unusual entrepreneurial prowess. Thirteen years passed from Joseph's sale into slavery until he stood self-assured, but shed of his pomposity, before the ruler of Egypt as Pharaoh's chief steward.

Nor did Joseph forget his spiritual inclinations. Pharaoh informed Joseph that the empire's destinies were in the hands of Joseph's God. Indeed, God had revealed to Joseph and thus to Pharaoh, the need to plan for times of drought and famine.

Although Pharaoh dallied with traditional Egyptian deities and their priests, Pharaoh praised Joseph openly. "Can we find anyone like this man, one in whom is the Spirit of God?" With Pharaoh's open blessing, Pharaoh began to entrust to this Hebrew former slave, the powers and prestige of empire. Hear the words of the Bible:

JOSEPH IN PRISON

Jacob's son Joseph – the special son – was jailed. His brothers tired of him lording it over them. They resented Jacob's favouritism. So they sold him to a travelling band of caravaners. Resold to an Egyptian servant in Potiphar's household, he proved to be a most able and a most valued advisor in that Egyptian household. Potiphar's wife accused Joseph of attempting to seduce her when really it was the other way around. He resisted her and by so doing, angered his temptress. Falsely accused, Joseph was imprisoned.

Joseph's ability to interpret dreams put him in his brothers' bad books. In prison, however, his talent won him praise. He interpreted the dreams of two fellow inmates, one of whom would be executed and one reprieved. When released, the reprieved prisoner forgot about Joseph. However, when Egypt's Pharaoh was agonizingly troubled by a dream, the servant recommended Joseph to Pharaoh.

The dream came to haunt Pharaoh so that he had no relief. Only after some time elapsed did the butler share with the king that he was once familiar with a fellow who did interpret his dream accurately. This led to Joseph entering Pharaoh's court and interpreted a dream about seven years of a great harvest, followed by seven years of desperate drought in which there would be no harvest. Pharaoh commended Joseph and empowered him to prepare for the famine by storing grain for the hard times ahead. So Joseph gave instructions that storehouses be built. Pharaoh saw that this young man had gifts of leadership as well as the gift of dream interpretation. He decided to install Joseph in an office in his court to oversee the matter of the content of this dream.

JOSEPH IN COMMAND

Joseph certainly took full charge of Egypt. He was the prime minister while Pharaoh was the monarch. He had the king's trust and endorsement. When scripture first introduced Joseph he seemed to be a spoiled brat who elevated himself by putting down his elder brothers.

But the brat grew up, just as most teens do when they come to terms with real life. He served not only the king but the Creator who had endowed him with talents, courage and insights. His work in Egypt bought honour to the Hebrew people, until 400 years later, they ended up in Egypt's slave caste.

Joseph once interpreted the dream of Pharaoh that Egypt would experience seven years of an abundant harvest. His advice and counsel were to gather the harvests in and store them for the future.

He also warned that hard times were to follow the boom times. A humungous famine would follow as long as the years of providential harvests. He saw to it that all of this was done, store for the bad times, use the boom to cover the bust. Obviously he was a manager of some courage, fortitude and ability. The people under his command and leadership responded and obeyed him.

What really does all of this tell a reader? First it tells us not to evaluate anyone at first glance. Secondly, we can see the benefit of his good management of resources. Would that modern politicians planned so well! Thirdly, and most important is that God had given him a unique place in history, for God's purposes and for the benefit of all the Hebrew people.

JACOB'S DYSFUNCTIONAL FAMILY

If you live in a dysfunctional family, take courage. A biblical über-hero lived in a family that was a mess. That's one great thing about the Bible, its heroes have clay feet and we see them vulnerable and pathetic at times. Yet they exhibit faith that overcomes distress.

Joseph, the one with the technicolour dream coat, was Jacob's pet son. He and Benjamin, were born to Jacob's wife, Rachel. Other brothers were born to Jacob's wife, Leah. Joseph's father could not hide his favouritism. Rachel was more loved than Leah, Rachel's children more than Leah's. Jacob demonstrated this both verbally and visually – such as the coat of many colours. Joseph's star waxed larger and larger in his father's galaxy.

The brothers tired of "put downs" no longer. They talked at first of killing Joseph, but demurred. Joseph showed remarkable maturity through a period of slavery, and a term of imprisonment, false accusations and injustice. Then he found favour in Pharaoh's court, becoming his prime minister, his chief economist and agricultural planner.

Soon the brothers arrived in Egypt to avoid a famine. Unknowingly they found themselves before Egypt's prime minister, their brother Joseph. Years had passed. The brothers knew not Joseph; but he knew them. In time Joseph revealed himself to them. When they begged his forgiveness he said, "Don't be distressed or angry with yourselves for selling me here because it was to save lives that God sent me ahead of you."

The brothers deed was inexcusable. That Joseph's grace and forgiveness covered it was remarkable.

"So Pharaoh said to Joseph, 'I hereby put you in charge of the whole land of Egypt,' Then Pharaoh took his signet ring from his finger and put it on Joseph's finger. He dressed him in robes of fine linen and put a gold chain around his neck. He had him ride in a chariot as his second-in-command, and men shouted before him, 'Make way!' Thus he put him in charge of the whole land of Egypt."

Meanwhile, back in Canaan, Jacob's dysfunctional family was also victim of the famine for which Joseph had been preparing in Egypt. Egypt's silos were filled with food, enough to carry through many years' drought – and word of Egypt's resources spread far and wide until Jacob's sons also heard of it, the same sons who years previously, had sold Joseph to Ishmaelite caravans *en route* from Gilead to Egypt. Think of the irony of the situation, but consider even more the magnanimity of Joseph who rose above the temptation of revenge.

As events developed, the very brothers who sold their brother to a trade caravan, found themselves in the bread line, as it were, standing before Pharaoh's second-in-command petitioning him for relief. Yet, they did not recognize Joseph.

For the time being, the descendants of Abraham were saved from starvation by one of their clan. Joseph, in fact, proposed that it was God's plan for him to be there, that things work out for good to those who love the LORD. Joseph persuaded his brothers that in the providence of God he had been sent on ahead of them to learn stewardship and plan agriculture, so that God's special family could be rescued from starvation and want.

Little did either Joseph or his brothers know what lay ahead for their people in Egypt. During their stay in Egypt they were welcome. After all, Joseph had bought for

JOSEPH AND FORGIVENESS

If ever Joseph had reason to renounce forgiveness, he had reason now. How could he forgive the maltreatment he suffered at his brothers' hands? Did his family really care about what happened to him? In this scenario few could ask how gracious they would be in forgiving if they had endured similar abuse. Answer – love! Love changed everything. He did not ask for justice, only a settlement of dealing with extreme hurt. Joseph had a special affection for his younger brother Benjamin whom he had not seen during his Egyptian sojourn.

Joseph created a special plan to find his younger brother and then to see him again. The biblical story, tells it in an intricate but delightful way. The brothers who had come some distance could scarcely believe that Joseph whom they pulled out of a cistern pit near Dothan in Canaan, could be free and then rise to high office of Egypt's Pharaoh.

Never losing his disguise, Joseph bartered with them by questioning them as to their real need and setting up a ploy that he might truly discover if his father and family were well.

Ultimately they returned to Egypt with their father and with Benjamin, the much beloved brother, and made arrangements that as long this famine continued, Egypt promised to meet their needs. Joseph in charge – he enabled the life of the Hebrew people to survive.

Forgiveness changes colour when care, love and foresight are all wrapped up in the phrase "forgiveness." This is the forgiveness that Joseph offered his family who had so miserably treated him.

Pharaoh all the lands of the peoples, in exchange for a 20% payment per year from all the crops they grew. Only the pagan priests' lands were not given over to Pharaoh. But times pass, and so do pharaohs.

In the succeeding years, the emperor's kindly dealings with Joseph and his descendants dwindled in direct proportion to the growing numbers of Hebrews in the land. Time came also when Pharaoh – possibly Sethos I – was no longer interested in Joseph's God. As the Bible says: "Then a new king, who did not know Joseph, came to power in Egypt. 'Look,' he said to his people, 'the Israelites have become much too numerous for us. Come, we must deal shrewdly with them or they will become even more numerous and, if war breaks out, will join our enemies, fight against us, and leave the country.'

"So they put slave masters over them to oppress them with forced labour, and they built Pithom and Ramases (in northeast Egypt) as store cities for Pharaoh. But the more they were oppressed, the more they multiplied and spread; so the Egyptians came to dread the Israelites and worked them savagely.

"They made their lives bitter with hard labour in brick and mortar and with all kinds of work in the fields; and in all their hard labour the Egyptians used them ruthlessly."

The ruins of storage warehouses may be seen near the Ramaseum, near Luxor. These "store cities" were dedicated to Atum, the Egyptian idea of a creator God, lord of the world, principle deity in the Egyptian closet of gods, an associated with the god Re, venerated in the setting sun.

During all this time something was happening to the children of Israel. They were growing together as community and in faith even while in persecution. They knew they were different than the Egyptians in ideals, faith

PHARAOH AND JOE WHO

Egypt, not Canaan, allowed the children of Abraham to become a nation. Nation-building was not in the Promised Land but in Egyptian slavery and escape. God provided a desert venue to established his people, known as the Israelites. The Ten Commandments explained; "And God spake all these words saying: `I am the Lord thy God, which have brought thee out of the land of Egypt, out of the house of bondage, thou shalt have no other Gods before me."'

Exodus begins with a story of the baby Moses, saved from the cruel Egyptian edict that all Israelite boy babies should die. One of Pharaoh's daughters intervened by rescuing the child and raising him as her own right in the palace! Moses grow up in the royal precinct, and enjoyed a royal education.

Moses spent 40 years exiled in the land of Midian, near the volcanic Mount Horeb. He had fled there from Egypt after killing an Egyptian who attacked an Israelite. As Moses pastured sheep in the shadow of the sacred mountain, a Voice from a fiery bush summoned Moses. The Voice, self-identified itself as YAHWEH, the God of Abraham, Isaac and Jacob, ordered Moses to return to Egypt. God instructed a reluctant Moses to identify himself as God's spokesman for both the Israelites and to Pharaoh the king.

Moses was negotiator – priest – between God and Pharaoh. He establish the supremacy of God and led the Israelite slaves to freedom. Under God's guidance, Moses reluctantly accepted the task. His royal upbringing gave him an edge, even in language before Pharaoh. Progressively powerful plagues from God's hand, inflicted the Egyptians, proved the might of God to both Pharaoh and the Israelites. This led to the Hebrews' escape from Egypt and slavery.

and heritage. And from their period of slavery and drudgery, they absorbed a great deal more than they realized about how they would become God's people.

Israelites escaped Pharaoh and Egypt thanks to the 10 plagues sent by God. The final plague, death of each Egyptian first-born son, drove Pharaoh to release all Israelite slaves. The dramatic Passover (*Pessach*) story of their escape, their crossing of the *yam suph* (Red or Reed Sea) is told in Exodus and in the *Haggada*, created centuries later that relates how Jews may celebrate the *seder*, the keeping of the Passover tradition.

In the next chapter we will note how the Egyptians prepared the Israelites and unwittingly offered them "godspeed," as they moved from their land of oppression, through the lessons they needed to learn to become a united nation under God.

CHAPTER 4

DEGRADATION AMID MONUMENTS

In the previous chapter we noted the Hebrew people – the "children of Israel" – moved from being welcome guests in Egypt to becoming a security problem. Egypt's power waxed and waned – and as it did, other ethnic groups, such as the Hyksos to the north, became a threat to Egypt. There came a point when Pharaoh and his leaders, concerned about their own security, saw potential danger in the numerical growth of the Israelites.

What if the Israelites formed an alliance with the Hyksos or other growing world powers, and became moles, or secret agents for the enemy?

So the Hebrew people lost their privileged status in Egypt. Not only that, they lost their freedom. Soon they were unwilling serfs building supply cities for Pharaoh in ancient Egypt.

PYRAMIDS

Egypt was ruled by Pharaohs from about 3,000 BC to Cleopatra's reign a few years before Jesus' birth. Pharaoh means "great house." It was an appropriate title, for the great house was an absolute monarch. His great house ultimately developed into the pyramids, in addition to the royal palace. All Egyptians considered their pharaohs to be deities as well as humans. He (rarely she) had the power of life and death over all subjects.

In death the pharaoh was embalmed or mummified. The body was ceremoniously paraded to its final resting

---

place. For about 500 years, from 2630 to 2150 BC, the pharaohs were buried in huge stone structures – pyramids.

The greatest of the pyramids at Giza contains 2.3 million stone blocks ranging in size from 2.5 to 15 tons. Thousands of slaves toiled for over 20 years to build the great pyramid. Its height, 150 meters exceeds the Statue of Liberty or St. Paul's Cathedral in London.

During flooding season along the Nile, field hands were press-ganged for tomb building. The pyramid's shape recreated the mound on which the sun god Amun-Re stood when he brought the other gods into existence.

A series of shafts or tunnels inside the pyramid led to numerous chambers. Some of these were used as storerooms for goods and treasures the king would need in the next world. Other passageways were meant to confuse and mislead grave robbers. The pyramids were built not as monuments but for stepping stones to the afterlife.

The pharaohs hoped that their spirits would return to claim the body for its journey to the after life. Unless the body was embalmed, the pharaoh could not journey to his next life. He needed sufficient provisions for the spiritual journey.

Every resource in the king's treasury was committed to this purpose. Obviously, the ancients sensed that there was more to life than the present.

Many of the mysteries of ancient Egypt came to light only after the discovery in 1797 of a decoder known as the Rosetta Stone. The languages written on it in Egyptian hieroglyphics, Demontic and Greek, allowed Egyptologists to decipher the meaning of the hieroglyphics. Since nearly all sculpture was produced for religious purposes, we are

EGYPTIAN RELIGION

Egyptians made no distinction between secular and sacred. All was sacred to them. Their society was from the top down, and the pyramid is a marvellous metaphor for Egyptian life. The king (emperor, pharaoh) was a deity and at the top. Serfs, slaves and peasants were at the base.

High in the top down pyramid, priests, princes and government officials took their places. The pharaoh was responsible not only for running the country but also for the rising and setting of the sun. What a responsible job!

Egyptian religion was complex. In its most primitive form it was characterized by a system of male and female deities. Each local settlement worshipped its own deity. These gods were often shaped like animals or birds.

Horus, for example, was often pictured as a hawk, and Bastet the daughter of Re, and the goddess of ripened crops, appeared as a cat.

The chief task of the priests was to enlist the help of the gods in the struggle against the forces of chaos.

All the language and imagery about this struggle reflected the Egyptian experience of the nature cycles of sun and river. Without the life-giving power of the sun and the waters of the Nile the people would perish.

For the Egyptians black was the colour of life. It represented the fertile earth deposited each year by the river as it flooded the vast low lying deltas. The silt of the Nile was the life blood of the nation and control of these cycles was a matter of life and death.

Sun and water were prominent themes in Egyptian religion, for without either, the crops would never grow.

able to learn of the gradual movement from the early Egyptians' worship of heavenly bodies and earthly objects. Their religion progressed and simplified until at some stages, it dabbled with monotheism.

The power bases for the pharaohs moved between the Lower Nile region and the Upper Nile. In the Upper Nile, the power base was in two of the supply cities, Tanis and Pithom and perhaps also at Memphis. In Memphis the evidence of Pharaoh's influence is evidenced by the statues of Rameses II which have been resurrected from burial in the sands of time.

Whereas the story of the Israelites and the Egyptians takes place almost exclusively in the Nile Delta, the most impressive of the Egyptian temples is in the Upper Nile region. This area was named Thebes by the Greeks but we know the area now by the names of Luxor and Karnak. Thebes West became the place of burial of the Pharaohs, each one entombed for the purpose of preparing for a future resurrection.

Thebes West was situated so that the morning light would reach into the temples guarding the pharaohs' mummified bodies. Thebes East, or Karnak, became the worship centres of the living Egyptian religions, but Karnak's temples were only for the priests' use not the people.

The reliefs in Karnack's temples depict the victories in Canaan by Sethos I and Rameses II, and show a king in his chariot. Around him are heaps of dead and wounded. The inhabitants of Canaan beg for mercy.

Into this setting of Egyptian power and Israelite powerlessness came one to free the people called Hebrews. His name was Moses. Born to a Hebrew family, this son of Israel escaped the infanticide imposed by the Egyptians upon

Hebrew male babies. He was in fact, adopted by Pharaoh's daughter in a ruse which allowed Moses to be reared in an Israelite faith while he became savvy in the Egyptian's political process. When he was discovered as being Hebrew, and when the death of an Egyptian taskmaster was laid at his feet, Moses escaped Egypt to Sinai. There, the severe lessons of the desert

---

MEANING OF THE NAME: YAHWEH

YAHWEH (YHWH) derived from the Semitic root HAWAH means "to be" and is translated as "the one who is" and "the one who causes to be." He is the Sustainer. Combined with God's claim to be the same God as worshipped by Moses' ancestors the name becomes better understood as, "the God who is always present."

The Israelite's God was not restricted to any particular boundary. Their God was worshipped anywhere and everywhere. He was the creator of the universe. He was all perfect, all knowing, eternal and holy. He had no physical form, no image and therefore had no name.

He was YHWH – "the one who is." No name could describe or contain the majesty of their God. He led his people to accept and believe in two basic ideas; that the Israelites were God's chosen people and; that the covenant at Mount Sinai moulded Israel into a nation with YAHWEH as King.

All law was made by YAHWEH In Israel. It was of divine origin, not human. YHWH, as he spoke to Moses from the burning bush, when asked what was his name, answered – "I am who I am." YAHWEH – the God who is and always will be. (Note: many versions of the Bible often use "Sovereign LORD" and not YAHWEH)

combined with the solitude of contemplation schooled him to be liberator of his people.

Like it or not, during their Egyptian sojourn, the Hebrew people learned how to be, as Jacob had said to Joseph, "a community of peoples." They grew together in faith, began to comprehend the revelations of the God who claimed them as his special people, and gradually coalesced in purpose, ethnicity, social mores and self-understanding.

In the desert of Sinai, Moses had learned much about his God, the God who would overcome the problems of the Hebrew people. At the burning bush, Moses learned first the name of his God – YAHWEH. It was a name so sacred, that few dared to repeat it aloud.

During this period of wandering, having escaped Egypt, the people had no government, no laws and no firm standards. But for them, Moses was able to provide all these needs through the communication he had with the God who met him on the holy mountain and instructed him for the benefit of his people. The Ten Commandments are no less than the highest form of lawgiving that has ever been devised.

BEDROCK LAWS: THE TEN COMMANDMENTS

When Moses led his people from their Egyptian slavery, Israel was but a collection of tribes, all of which was held tenuously together in a religious federation. What was held commonly by all was their commitment to the LORD.

At Sinai, God and Moses made another covenant. Central to it were stipulations known as "The Ten Words" (*deka logous*). We now call them the Ten Commandments. Some have thought of them as the ten suggestions, but not Moses or his people.

Why ten? Perhaps because we have ten fingers! They represent totality and completeness of the laws. They touch every aspect of life. The drama of the lawgiving underlined their importance. Moses descended the mountain of the LORD with two stone slabs, with the laws "written by the finger of God," imbedded in them.

These commandments contained principles of living which were fundamental to all future legislation by Israel. They stipulated the obligations of Israel toward God.

The Ten Words, or principles, began with the worth and worship of God ("worth" derives from worship). That was primary. The next three commandments indicated how the one God – YAHWEH – was properly to be worshipped.

The remaining six commandments set the bounds for relationships with others. Look after your parents and those who can't look after themselves. Murder is not allowed. Sexual faithfulness is expected. The home must be protected. Honesty is required and ownership must be honoured. Society must have freedom from theft. Framing someone in a court of law or by character assassination is forbidden. Expect the truth. You must not covet what belongs to someone else. Freedom from envy is a requirement.

Obviously, these laws were exceedingly foundational. They are bedrock laws. Every modern civilized nation builds its legal system upon them. In this way, the tribes of Israel, consenting to this covenant made between themselves and their LORD became the givers of enlightened society for the modern world.

Traditional Mount Sinai has been venerated for hundreds of centuries. Among those attracted to these austere surroundings were pilgrims and ascetics who sought this place as a locale suited for private devotion. It became a settlement of Christian monks.

The magnificent fortress – St. Catherine's Monastery – signifies many biblical traditions. It is the traditional location of Mount Sinai where Moses received the Ten Commandments. It also celebrates a cave of Elijah who came here and heard God speaking to him in a "still, small voice."

SAINT CATHERINE'S MONASTERY

St. Catherine's monastery marks the traditional site of Moses' burning bush. By the third century it became a refuge for persecuted Christians, a stopover for travellers and a home for hermits.

Local tribesmen still menaced these ascetic Christian monks three centuries later. About 300 monks lived there by that time. Emperor Justinian built them the present monastery to provide them some safety.

The ancient basilica built in 542 AD is at the centre of the monastery. The doors are made of Lebanese cedar. The interior is decorated with marble, mother of pearl, icons, murals, mosaics and hanging lamps.

A rare sixth century mosaic of the transfiguration is in the library. The walled complex protects a treasury of rare books. Rare icons are displayed in the apse. Also to be found here is The Chapel of the Burning Bush. Some relics of the fourth century martyr Saint Catherine are also situated within St. Catherine's protective walls.

For the faithful members of this community, death was a beginning, not the end of life. The earthly remains of former monks are not a macabre display but a silent witness to the faith of those who have predeceased the current monks.

KONSTANTIN VON TISCHENDORF

Emperor Justinian contracted to build St. Catherine's Monastery in the Sinai at the foot of Mt. Gebel Musa – Moses' mountain. An earlier chapel, built by Emperor Constantine's mother, Helena, was set here. She determined that this location was where Moses received the Law.

The monks named the place after St. Catherine of Alexandria who was alleged to have been tortured on the wheel (The Catherine Wheel). She died in the process, and for her faith in Jesus, her Saviour. Justinian intended that the 80-foot walls protect the monks from marauding Bandits. They did.

In the mid-1800s, a visitor to St. Catharine's discovered the fruit of the labours of the monks' work of copying and recopying biblical manuscripts. Some manuscripts in the Monastery predate the fortress itself.

The visitor to the monastery was Konstantin von Tischendorf, a very capable scholar from Leipzig whose aim was to produce a new version of the New Testament based on the oldest manuscripts. His search for such manuscripts brought him to St. Catherine's.

In May, 1844, Tischendorf discovered some monks feeding a fire with old velum paper. He wrote: "What was my surprise to find amid this heap of papers a considerable number of sheets of a copy of the Old Testament in Greek, which seemed to me, to be one of the most ancient I had ever seen." The scholar had found Codex Sinaiticus.

Tischendorf "saved" the manuscripts which now reside in the British Museum. How they got there is another story. He asked the monks if he could "borrow" the manuscripts and after much waiting and getting permission,

ARK OF THE COVENANT

The Israelites had no image of God, but within a small rectangular box (the Ark) the Israelites placed their greatest treasure, the stone tablets on which were written the Ten Words God gave to Moses.

God specified its exact size, shape and materials from which the Ark was to be constructed. Made of acacia wood lined inside with gold and covered with gold outside. A gold slab was on top. On either side stood two cherubim. This was understood as God's throne. God met and spoke with Moses from between two decorative angels. The Ark prompted the Israelites of their covenant with God and his nearness to them. It reminded them of God's requirements on all aspects of their lives. God was all-present.

Priests carried the Ark from place to place as the Israelites moved toward their promised land. At rest, the Ark was a place where the people could come to seek God's will for them. Although God remained invisible to his people, it represented the mighty power of God which often manifested itself through the ark. Once the Israelites had settled in the promised land, the Ark was put in a special place for all to see. This was at a shrine called Shiloh.

Years after, the Philistines attacked Shiloh and captured the Ark. Shiloh soon lost its importance. The Israelites abandoned the Ark until David, after defeating the Philistines, retrieved the Ark and brought it to Jerusalem where it was placed in a tent in his palace gardens. The Ark disappeared during the fall of Jerusalem and the burning of the Temple in 586 BC. A symbol of this Ark is found today in every synagogue. Each Ark houses a copy of the Torah.

he presented them to Russia's Czar as a gift. When the Russian Revolution developed in 1917, the new government sold the manuscripts to the British Museum for needed money. As yet, the monks have not received back the manuscripts they "lent" to Konstantin von Tischendorf.

The monastery still claims the borrowed manuscripts. Nonetheless, St. Catherine's Monastery reminds us primarily of the Ten Commandments.

In Sinai the law was visualized by symbols so that the truths of the unseen law would be conspicuous. These symbols were kept in a sacred box which became known as the Ark of the Covenant.

Like most humans, the Israelites needed visibility in their faith structures. God provided that a place of worship be constructed in order for the people to sense that God was with them. The Tabernacle was a tent of meeting, and it was built within the camping grounds of the people themselves. God is holy and yet he was among them as one of them.

THE TABERNACLE

The Hebrew people first met God directly in the desert at Sinai. In Exodus, the Bible tells us that the people of Israel experienced a progressive revelation of YHWH which lasted 40 years. It continued as a place representing God's presence until Israel built a Temple. In some instances other shrines (e.g. Shiloh) served a similar purpose.

Above all else, they came to know him as a God who leads his people into their future. YAHWEH manifested himself through the appearance of a cloud by day and a pillar of fire by night. These symbols led the procession toward the promised land.

In this spiritual journey through the wilderness YAHWEH's people discover God is more than a trailblazer. He camps with them! God is not only everywhere, he lives among his people. In the fourth gospel John describes Jesus residency in similar terms (1:14). "The Word (Jesus) became flesh and pitched his tent in our campground."

The same God who has created everything, who has no beginning or end, opts to dwell with his people. In scriptural terms, God "tabernacles" among the people.

The Tabernacle housed the Ark of the Covenant, containing the tablets of the Law. This was God's house, the Divine dwelling. It symbolized God's presence, and assured Israel-in-waiting that God's favour rested on his people.

The Bible describes its construction. It began with a rectangular wooden frame 15 by 5 by 5 meters. At one end of this space was a smaller area called the "Holy of Holies" containing the Ark of the Covenant.

The larger area within the tent (the Holy Place) held the seven-branched (later nine-branched) candlestick and the table for the ceremonial shewbread. This same basic configuration was later transferred from the tabernacle or tent shrine to Solomon's Great Temple.

The tabernacle helped inform the peoples' understanding of God's nature. It revealed YAHWEH as an intimate God. He is neither remote nor unknowable. God freely chooses to meet us at the centre of human history and live within the "heart" of each human being. He came to dwell among us and pitches his tent with us.

Nothing in the religious tradition of their desert neighbours can explain this development. Clearly, this insight is a gracious gift of the God of Abraham, Isaac and Jacob to his people Israel.

The Tabernacle became the visible symbol of God's presence with his people. When the people moved, the Tabernacle moved with them. Through this symbol, God was telling his people that *he was with them* in their dust, desert and difficulties.

The people needed to know that the God who brought them out of Egypt would not abandon them in the wilderness. The Tabernacle was their tangible proof, that YAHWEH was always among his people. In our next chapter we shall see how communal faith and spirituality were fostered in the pilgrims' process, as faith seekers became faith finders.

CHAPTER 5

DEVELOPING INSTITUTIONS AND FUNDAMENTALS

As we concluded the previous chapter we noted that the wilderness period of 40 years was not spent in complete frustration. Rather this was an essential formative period of self-discovery for the descendants of Jacob also known as Israel – the Israelites.

Special days were also set aside to symbolize the acts of God among the people. Soon, in addition to the Passover, was the keeping of the Sabbath – Shabbat. As the people progressed toward the land they were to inhabit and reclaim, they celebrated festivals to remember the providence of God in the provision of food and water.

They always celebrated spiritual renewal each year as they came before God in confession and admission of their sins, to receive absolution and promises of God's mercy. So there developed, on the great Day of Atonement – *Yom Kippur* – the celebration of the scapegoat.

Their rituals were added to by the development of a priesthood. Aaron became the model human priest, and the offspring of their ancestor Levi were to be the priests of Israel in perpetuity.

Four hundred years in Egypt, followed by 40 years in the wilderness of Sinai served as the embryonic years of growing faith and developing government, of morals and ethics, and a spiritual enlightenment that no other nation on the face of the earth had seen.

During this period their worship experiences became learned routines which were familiar to them, their government-in-exile was formulated, their priesthood was

THE DAY OF ATONEMENT

Yom Kippur, the Day of Atonement, occurs on the tenth of Tishri. That day is devoted to self-examination, confession, and atonement. On the Day of Atonement the people rested and fasted. No work was done. The high priest, wearing garments special for the occasion performed appropriate rituals (Leviticus 16). This ritual cleansed the sanctuary of the Temple or Tabernacle of any impurity.

The High Priest offered two sin offerings on Yom Kippur, one for the priest, and one for the people. Sin offerings cleansed the sanctuary of impurity. A sin offering was regularly offered at festivals. God ordered Aaron to bring a young bullock as a sin offering and a ram as a burnt offering.

The priest brought bull's blood into the inner shrine, the Holy of Holies, where the Ark was kept. The high priest entered the Holy of Holies after placing a pan of burning incense inside to make a smoke screen between him and the Ark (Lev. 16:13). Aaron then sprinkled the blood of the bull and ram on the altar and mercy seat.

After cleansing the sanctuary the priest laid his hands on a second goat and confessed the people's sins. One goat was sacrificed for the Lord, the other for Azazel (or scapegoat). Thus the priest symbolically transferred the sins of the people to the goat, then drove it into the wilderness. This represented God's way of providing a means of atonement for his people. When the sanctuary or land became defiled, or when the people became unfaithful, confession followed by atonement removed the sinful barrier to the covenant relationship.

The Day of Atonement is the culmination of 10 days of repentance. It alone of all the Jewish holidays is the equivalent of Shabbat in sanctity.

BEGINNINGS OF THE PRIESTHOOD — WHAT IS A PRIEST?

From the most ancient times people have chosen someone to act as a mediator with their God. Jews, who worshipped the one true God, YHWH, from the earliest known times, left the role of priest to the first born male of their family. He was to speak to God on their behalf.

Later the role of the priest became more formal. A man chosen to perform priestly duties was said to be born to holiness, chosen by God. He was consecrated, that is, given over for life in the service of God.

His role was that of mediator and atoner. Priest means bridge. His function was to bridge God's people in meeting with God. He became the one chosen by God to offer sacrifice on behalf of all the people of Israel in atonement for their sins.

Jesus is the ultimate priest. He priested on behalf of humans with God. He is the high priest who offered the ultimate sacrifice for all time, for the sins of all humankind.

In the early Church, the community chose its leaders to gather people to praise and worship God. The early Church appointed and consecrated bishops (pastors) and deacons and later Presbyters (elders).

The word priest, or minister, has different meanings for different groups. For the Catholic and Orthodox churches, the priesthood follows closely the tradition of presiding over the sacrificial act of atonement (mass), albeit in an unbloody manner. For Protestant and other churches a priest's role is more of leader and teacher.

For all Christians, Jesus remains the one, holy priest whose sacrificial act made possible washing sin away.

THE LEVITICAL SYSTEM

Levites were generally, but not always, those who belonged to the tribe of Levi. Levi was the third son of Jacob by his wife Leah. In some biblical passages "Levite" appears to be descriptive rather than a tribal name.

Levites appear to be priests whose function was to offer sacrifices and administer the Torah. The role and responsibilities of Levites changed over many centuries. At one point they were demoted to being Temple servants, with a clear distinction made between priests and Levites. Post-exilic (after Judah returned from its exile after an absence of 70 years) developments greatly increased the role of Levites and restored much of their former importance.

During this exile, when the Temple was destroyed, Jews could not offer sacrifices. When the city wall was rebuilt under Nehemiah's direction, Levites adapted to newer reforms of their roles. They emphasized ritual purity and orderly religious activity.

Under this code of law all worship was to be conducted with proper solemnity by the priests. When priests offered sacrifices, the new code insisted that they take care to perform their offerings at a proper time, using prescribed rituals and prayers appropriate to the type of sacrifice involved.

Major sacrifices were re-instituted by returned exiles. Sacrifices once again were tied to the religious calendar. Religious leaders insisted on required pilgrimages to the Temple for major festivals. Priests enforced their authority. Proper observance of the Sabbath was important as one of those religious activities distinctive to Jews, and unparalleled by any other people in the ancient Near East.

initiated. Of the dozen tribal groups, one tribe alone was set aside for spiritual leadership – the Levites.

The very first institutional aspect of their soon-to-be-ritualized faith, was the Passover – *Pesach*. Passover celebrated how God spared the children of Israel. God did not spare the Egyptians from the ultimate plague of the firstborn which God visited upon the people of Egypt. That was because Pharaoh would not allow Moses to lead his people to freely worship their God in the desert. This family celebration was to remind them forever that their God was an overcomer who would lead them into selfhood and deliver them from their troubles.

The priestly group, including the Levites, were supported by a system of giving which some would call a tax. It was known as tithing. A tithe was a tenth, and so the first tenth of the income from every Israelite, was set aside to support the religious system. This was not to be considered as an offering but as a payment of a debt to God. The debt was to be the reminder that God alone was sovereign and that everyone needed that reminder so as to not be spiritually presumptuous.

In addition to the institution of a religious system, the Israelites also developed a highly respectable social justice system, the most advanced and fair system of any civilization to that date. The social system derived from the principles enunciated in the Ten Words, or Ten Commandments which were given by God to Moses on Mount Sinai.

During this time also, the people of Israel were able to reflect on how they had heard of God's leading from the spies, Joshua and Caleb. Their minority report had encouraged the entire community to possess the land. But lacking faith, and hearing conflicting reports from ten spies

WHAT THE SPIES SAW

The Hebrew people, under Moses' command, sent two spies to Canaan from their wilderness encampments to check the obstacles and benefits that might await their invasion of "The Promised Land."

A dozen men were commissioned to see and report back on what awaited them. Ten of them offered a majority report that they were intimidated by what they saw –"Giants in the land!" Two suggested that what others called problems were merely opportunities.

The 12 men made their way into the hill country by way of Be'ersheba and Hebron. How far into the land had they gone? No one knows. They travelled sufficiently far to realize that this truly was a prosperous land, "full of milk and honey." However, Canaan was also inhabited by the Anakim, otherwise described as "the lofty people."

To a people that were accustomed to labour and not to battle, nor to any prospect that there would be the need of hand to hand combat, the inhabitants of this land would seem to be too formidable a body. It is always easier to ridicule the weaker spies whose majority report that said "Invasion of the Promise Land is impossible." These reporters preferred returning to Egypt and its servitude than risk all the venture of following Moses.

There was the minority report. Two spies saw a land of promise as the fulfilment and satisfaction of their every desire and dream. They were people who believed, that if led of the LORD, they could well enjoy the prosperity and fruits of the land. Joshua and Caleb saw the dream and the vision – the others, who proved to be the majority, saw only giants who dwelt in the land.

ISRAEL'S LAWS OF SOCIAL JUSTICE

The Sinai Covenant stipulations formed the law of the nation. Any crime committed is against God, whether it be religious or civil. Israel perceives that all its law is divinely given. The Sinai Covenant is depicted as conditional; Israel must keep the stipulations such as familial, societal, dietary, ritual and agricultural, or suffer severe punishment.

Civil and religious law were the same."Torah," which means teaching or instruction, imposed penalties for crimes of theft, murder, adultery, as well as crimes against God such as blasphemy and pagan worship.

Hospitality was an overriding legal custom of pastoral nomads. Once hospitality was offered and accepted, hostilities were impossible until the parties parted and agreed upon a mutual truce period. From Exodus through the Settlement Period, social organization was based on the extended family. A man determined his lineage first by his father, then by his clan, his tribe, and perhaps his people. Focus was on family life. Villages organized into clusters of multiple-family compounds. Household heads were grandfather, or eldest active male member.

In matters of law, the head of the household exercised the powers of "pater familias." He could punish or reward without interference. If the head of a household wilfully broke the law he endangered the very survival of the community. His family group could be destroyed.

Beyond the household, village authority lay with elders who were the heads of households or property owners. They represented the community's wisdom. They dealt with cases which affected the entire community.

who recounted something different from the other two, a majority voted by voicing their fears to not go forward. When two say "go" and ten say "stop," should majority sensitivity win out over venture faith? It did then!

For the present the people elected to not invade. The result of that choice meant a longer gestation period in the birth of the nation. It was as if God said to them, "If you plan to fail, I'll let you succeed at failing!" Yet God led the people to further grow in community development, enabling them to set standards of community life and see that the interests of the weak, the sick and the unprotected should not be dismissed by a belief that "might is right."

When 40 years of desert development had passed, the people known as Israelites were ready to enter the land from which their ancestor Jacob and his sons left 400 years earlier for the food provided in Egypt. Moses was forbidden by God to enter the reclaimed and reconquered land because he had dared to not heed God's express command to him on one occasion. Moses said goodbye to his Israelite family and prepared to die on Mount Nebo, east of Jericho.

Joshua and Caleb, two of the spies who had encouraged the Israelites to invade and conquer, were permitted by God to lead the invasion. Hordes of Israelites gathered on the east bank of the Jordan River, ready to ford it and retake what they believed was rightfully theirs.

The first important beachhead was at Jericho, and the untested Israelite army prepared for its first-ever battle. Jericho was the oldest continuously inhabited city in the ancient world. If it fell to Israel, it would be a good omen.

The Israelite's lessons were learned the hard way. Jericho fell too easily. The Israelites soon learned that their next battle would teach them more diligence and humility. The Israelite army was beaten badly at Ai. When

INVASION OF JERICHO

The Children of Israel invaded Canaan from the east. That meant they had to cross the Jordan River. The inhabitants of walled Jericho could see them massing but were obviously daunted by their presence. When we read of this invasion, we read a story of psychological warfare.

Joshua replaced Moses as the leader. First he ordered the people to wash their utensils, clothing and themselves to ritually prepare for the invasion. "Sanctify yourselves, for tomorrow the LORD will do amazing things among you" (Joshua 3). The priests carrying the Ark led them followed by the soldiers.The priests carried rams' horns (shofars), while tooting them as they marched around Jericho six times in seven days without firing an arrow.

Seven priests carried the Ark and blew ram's horns. On the seventh day they circled the city seven times. On day seven all the people joined in this parade about the city and once the seventh circle had been made, those blowing the shofars gave a long blast, the people shouted, and the walls collapsed. Jericho was theirs.

Jericho has been the subject of numerous excavations. The mound or tel has seen extensive digging, but no specific finds have disclosed the specific victory of Joshua. Researchers have located prior cities and newer cities in the same place, however, some of which has found that inhabitants used mud-baked bricks used in walls.

The people who endured 40 years of wilderness waiting now had a foothold in their Land of Promise. The smooth invasion led to an immediate sense that the invasion would continue with the same ease. It did not. The people, but not Joshua, became overconfident.

the remnants of the army gathered to lick their wounds, it was discovered that some soldiers in the army had not followed God's orders and directives. Lesson number One: God's people were to follow God's commands to achieve God's victories. Joshua may have been Field Marshall but YAHWEH would always be "Commander-in-Chief."

Gradually the army and people moved northward to Galilee and westward towards the Mediterranean. They bypassed Salem, or Jerusalem, stronghold of the Jebusites. They camped midway in their mission, near a well once used by their ancestor Jacob, later to also supply water to Jesus. They paused briefly to recall that this soil was land promised by God to his obedient servant Abraham. Jacob's well was nearby Shechem where the wandering Aramean Abraham built his first altar to God. It was there that Joshua asked the people to recommit themselves to the Lord they served.

MOUNTS OF BLESSING AND CURSING

Two sacred mountains stand nearby the holy city of Shechem in central Samaria when the Israelites encamped travelling north. They are named Mount Gerezim, also known as "the mount of blessings," and Mount Ebal, "known as the "mount of curses." These are the Canaanite "Twin Peaks," if you like. Their importance goes back to Abraham, Isaac and Jacob. Joshua, the re-conqueror of the land, put Mounts Gerezim and Ebal into higher prominence.

Before Joshua would continue his conquest of Canaan, he asked the people of Israel he was leading to re-covenant with the LORD. They agreed. So he placed some of the people on the lower slopes of Mount Gerezim and some across the valley on the lower slopes of Mount Ebal.

As he read out the benefits of following the LORD's commands, the people on Mount Gerezim shouted "Amen!" Then as he read out the negatives which would come from disobeying the covenant, the people on Mount Ebal shouted "Amen!" And so it continued until all the blessings of the law, and every curse for breaking the covenant was recited by all the people.

Seven hundred years later, when Samaritans had intermarried with Assyrian settlers, the Jews returning from exile would not allow the Samaritans to help rebuild Jerusalem's walls or its Temple. So the Samaritans, resentful of the insult to them by Nehemiah, countered by building their own temple atop Mount Gerizim.

When Jesus paused at Jacob's Well, just below Mount Gerezim, the woman who drew water for him to drink reminded him that Samaritans worshipped God here at Gerezim.

Jesus countered, "God is Spirit. The time is coming when true worshippers will worship God in Spirit and in Truth. For such the Father seeks to worship him" (John 4:24 *ff*).

Having rededicated themselves to God, the armies of Joshua and Caleb launched an attack on the northern part of Canaan, in what is called the Galilee. In the hills of Upper Galilee was a mighty city guarded by a mighty fortress.

Hazor was an erudite city of considerable culture and influence. It was the lead city in the north of Israel. It stood as a stronghold guarding trade routes, and therefore taxation routes to the east and west, and to the northern slopes of Mount Hermon, not far away. Joshua launched a furious attack on Hazor and in effect, consolidated the geographical extremities of the Canaanite federation as Israel's own territory.

THE INVASION OF HAZOR

Hazor was a fortified city which guarded the route between Lower and Upper Galilee. It was settled by Canaanite people and reached a high level for a civilized society. Judging from the late bronze age art and imported Mycenaean pottery found there, it was a maturing city of arts and crafts.

Its importance included the fact that Hazor had a spring inside its urban centre. In turn, the dependable supply of potable water meant that it could withstand a protracted siege from most enemies.

Evidently the Egyptian king, Pharaoh Seti I, attacked and destroyed Hazor some time between 1318 and 1300 BC. Its citizens rallied quickly to rebuild Hazor.

Professor Yigael Yadin, who excavated Hazor, dates the invasion of Joshua's army in the late 1200s. The pottery debris found at Hazor could only have been created after 1300 BC. Yadin concluded that Hazor was the largest city of its day in Canaan, and populated by 40,000 people.

There was evidence that Joshua's conquest of Hazor was violent. In the area of the Stelae Temple, were found overturned slabs which demonstrated the temple's violent destruction. Signs of a firestorm, powdery ash and charred beams gave evidence of what the Bible related about Joshua's battle at Hazor: "Yet Israel did not burn any of the cities built on their mounds – except Hazor, which Joshua burned . . . So Joshua did it; he left nothing undone of all that the LORD commanded Moses."

The Israelite conquest of Hazor was a frantic orgy of smashing and intemperate destruction without compromise. When Yadin's excavators dug into the rubble, they found some exciting evidence of a Canaanite shrine. The temple was equipped with an incense altar, a large basalt basin, earthenware jars, and propriety symbols of Canaanite worship including a figure of the Canaanite storm-god Hadad on a bull.

By this time Joshua was a senior citizen. Joshua had left Egypt as slave, endured the wilderness as a compatriot and lieutenant of Moses and, then as a strategist, led the remnant of Israel – plus its new generation – into Canaan to repossess it.

But time ran out for this great warrior and nation builder. Joshua's name means Saviour; he had saved his people and brought them home again. His work was done.

As we shall see in the next chapter, some of the lessons which the people of Israel learned in the desert needed to be taught all over again. They needed to refocus on God, reform their unity and learn to cope with those people whose way of life and attitudes were in great spiritual contrast to themselves.

CHAPTER 6

TITLE TO CANAAN

As we noted in the previous chapter, leaders such as Joshua are few and far between. Joshua had special skills of organization, coupled with street savvy and unusual spiritual depth. He also had a rich insight into his own purpose in life and was not drawn away from it.

Joshua's forces had won the battle, and had reconquered the land – but did not win the peace. After Joshua's death the spiritual foundations, seemingly set so securely by Joshua, began to crumble. The land of promise originally was divided into 12 regions, one for each tribal unit of Israelites.

For a while, all the 12 tribes together formed Israel and they became united as a monarchy. However, the tribal boundaries changed and the land of promise was divided under two kings. The two southern tribes formed the nation of Judah; the ten northern tribes formed the nation of Israel.

In a land where no law was honoured, everyone proposed his own law. As the biblical book of Judges records, "In those days, Israel had no king; everyone did as he saw fit."

From time to time a small luminary for justice and righteousness lit a tiny area of the land. As we shall see, after Moses' father-in-law gave him advice to appoint judges, the role of judge in Israel was helpful to the running of the nation. After Joshua's time, the role of judge took on a new and special significance.

Rules and regulations were more or less adhered to in Israel's fledgling judicial system. However, a national

JOSHUA / JESUS (SAVIOUR)

The first chapter of Matthew's gospel, in the New Testament records that an angelic messenger spoke to Joseph, engaged to Mary: "Joseph, be not afraid to take Mary to be your wife. For it is by the Holy Spirit that she has conceived. She will have a son, and you will name him Jesus – because he will save his people from their sins."

Names have origins. The name Jesus comes from the Latin by way of the Greek language. The Greek name Jesus is a translation of the Hebrew name Joshua, which means "He shall save."

Joshua is a mighty name in the history of God's chosen people. For it was Joshua who led the children of Israel, after their wandering in the desert for 40 years, into the promised land.

His final challenge rolls down through the ages: "Choose you this day, whom you will serve. As for me and my house, we will serve the LORD." Jesus, of course, was to be another kind of Saviour. Joshua was a contraction of Yehoshuah meaning "YHWH will save."

Jesus was not an exclusive name by any means. Josephus, the Roman historian of the time, mentions at least 19 persons named Jesus. In the gospels, particularly after Peter's declaration "You are the Christ," Jesus is most often addressed as Lord or Teacher, sometimes as Master or Rabbi, rarely by the name Jesus.

Christ, the chosen one, the anointed of God becomes his identity. Jesus Christ, that title indicates one chosen and appointed to be the Saviour. It was his identity down through the ages, the theology of his person, his attributes and his mission.

ROLE OF THE JUDGES

Moses, at the suggestion of his father-in-law, Jethro, appointed the first Judges.They assisted Moses in executing his duties. Moses was weighed down with the onus of guiding Israelites in their everyday lives. He needed help both in making judgments and administering the Law.

The first Judges were chosen by Moses to assist him in this mammoth task. These earlier Judges held sessions under palm trees. Their justice was simple and swift. Other Judges, in later years were more charismatic leaders rather than arbitrators and mediators.

Israelite law was created by YHWH, God himself. Because the Torah was seen to be of divine origin all other aspects of law, social, economic etc. were also were seen as being divinely ordained.

Judges mediated between YHWH and his people as they lived out their everyday lives. For the Israelites, coming from the wilderness to the promised land of Canaan, this was a time for creating a new society.

Gradually the Israelites took over control of the land, the economy, even the laws of the land. Tensions rose, especially in matters concerning worship. YHWH vied with the pagan gods.

Finally, Israel was forced to define its laws; political, secular and religious. Nevertheless, local tribes fought constant battles with themselves.

The tribes needed stronger hands to guide them. Thus God allowed his people to be led and governed by judges. Judges were interim leaders to oversee the divided tribes as they progressed toward a peaceful nation founded on YAHWEH's commandments.

CITIES OF REFUGE

The Levites, Temple servants, were given no special territory after the conquest of Canaan. Rather, they were allocated 48 cities surrounded by pasture land. Six of these were to be cities of refuge – three in Canaan and three east of the River Jordan. They were cities of refuge for the people of Israel, as well as strangers and sojourners among them.

The Cities of Refuge were administered by the Levites, men acquainted with the law who possessed a judicial temperament. The right of asylum is a common institution in all times and places. Greeks, Romans and others through the Middle Ages valued sanctuaries of refuge. The custom is found even from the time of barbarian people. At first, any shrine afforded sanctuary. Later, when worship was more centralized, Israelites found other "arks."

The Torah does not offer sanctuary to every killer, but only to ones who unknowingly or unintentionally take a life. This provision is moral and humane. Avengers alternatively, rather than take life for life could collect debts, contract a levirate marriage, or redeem a kinsman's slave.

General rules guided a community to distinguish the murderers from those guilty only of manslaughter. A killer using any instrument, whether of iron, stone or wood convicted the killer of murderous intent. This released him from sanctuary. Avengers usually executed murderers.

The law provided instructions about previous hatred or premeditation, revealing murderous intent. If the killer was guilty of any of these he must die at the hands of the avenger. If the killing occurred, however, without premeditation, or by accident, the slayer was protected from the avenger by being kept in the city of refuge.

legal uniformity did not exist – Israel lacked a central government. Some laws seemed harsh, but the laws contained a large measure of compassion. An example of the justice system's provision for clemency is shown by the establishment of cities of refuge.

With Joshua's demise, weaker Israelite leaders could not hold back the persistent Canaanites. The Canaanites were not a fledgling nation like Israel and for that reason had somewhat more experience in adjusting to the peculiarities of boundary changes which occurred so frequently in that area of the earth. The Canaanites made bad neighbours because they caused the Israelites to retreat spiritually from the high level of trusting the God who had decreed that Abraham's offspring should be a blessing to the nations. The opposite happened. Israel was polluted in its faith by its neighbours.

One of the judges who was motivated to contend with the neighbours of the newly conquered Canaan was Ehud the Benjaminite. Ehud not only kept his faith, but took it upon himself to assassinate the king of Moab who had attacked Jericho and captured it from the newly settled Israelites. Ehud, known as "the left-handed," led an attack against Moab and won a victory. But as the Bible says, "After Ehud died, the Israelites once again did evil in the sight of the LORD."

SOME OF THE JUDGES

Deborah was another of the so-called "judges" who gave interim leadership between the death of Joshua and the development of Israel's monarchy. Deborah was called a "prophetess." She presided in the area of Beth-el, but earned a reputation as the leader who assassinated Sisera, the prime

CANAANITES

Israelites arriving at their promised land knew it was already occupied. The principal group was another Semitic people, the Canaanites. Mixed in with them were other non-semites such as the Hittites and Horites.

Canaanites were semi-bonded in several city states primarily along the coastline of Palestine and in pockets in the central Shephela mountains. They paid tribute to the Pharaohs of Egypt. Their religion had developed independently from Egypt and more closely resembled fertility faiths.

They worshipped a pantheon of gods who were thought to dwell on a mountain in the north. The best known divinity was Baal, who is mentioned in the history books as one of the local Canaanite idols, representing male fertility. Baal's female counterpart was the goddess Asherah, deriving perhaps from fertility moon worship in Ur. These gods could be born, die, marry and beget children.

Canaanite religious writings reflected bloody conflict between life forces and chaos. In the end, the evil forces were overcome by the fertile union of male and female aspects to produce new life. The religion of the Canaanites found its focus in ritual prostitution. Shrine bordellos were attached to the temples and staffed by women consecrated to the goddess of fertility.

Although the Torah condemns Baal worship and its cultic prostitution, clearly Israel did borrow from Canaanite religion, and transformed items into YHWH worship. Some Canaanite texts reappear unchanged in the writings of the Torah. Their temple sanctums became architectural templates for Jerusalem's Temple.

general of Canaanites who had retaken Hazor. So successful was Deborah, that the Bible records, "Then the land had peace for 40 years."

Famous also was a judge named Gideon. The Bible reveals that the Israelites had taken to the "mountain clefts, caves and strongholds" watching their powerful neighbours, the Midianites. On camels, the Midianites trampled out the crops every time they were planted.

Gideon received a revelation that he was to restore the honour of the LORD among the people. So, sensing that Gideon was a true warrior and champion of YAHWEH, the people rallied to defeat the Midianites. Their battle cry was, "The sword of the LORD and of Gideon." Again the Bible states the consequences: "Thus Midian was subdued before the Israelites and did not raise it's head again. During Gideon's lifetime, the land enjoyed peace 40 years."

Jephthah, child of a prostitute, first led a group of brigands, then, because he demonstrated good leadership, was made a leader of his tribe in Gilead for about six years. His exploits were limited but he did recall his people from the idolatry they had come to practise, into obedience of YAHWEH.

Among the neighbour nations to most disturb the Israelites were a people called Philistines. History often has done them a disservice. "Philistine" has come to mean "boorish." Actually the Philistines were more advanced in many ways than were the Israelites who came to detest them. Philistines knew about iron tools and weapons whereas Israel was using bronze. Philistines had developed art forms, usually associated with their religion, a practice forbidden by the Ten Commandments.

Among those who did battle with the Philistines was the legendary Samson. He too was a "judge" of Israel.

Samson's life was lived out among the Philistine people, the coastal group of settlers with Phoenician background. The Philistines arrived along the Mediterranean coastline about the same time as the Israelites and became their nemesis. Samson received strength beyond belief.

Called a Nazarite, this child was never to shave nor use intoxicating beverages. If *only* he kept his vow . . . ! Samson never lived up to his billing as either a political or spiritual leader. He was physically strong but spiritually weak. Although he was a judge of questionable success, his exploits became folk stories retold around the dinner tables as fathers regaled their sons about the history of their people.

Israelites living amid the Philistines conformed to the idolatry of Baal. The Bible records, "Again the Israelites did evil in the eyes of the LORD, so the LORD delivered them into the hands of the Philistines for 40 years."

Within this period Samson was born to a villager named Manoah from the tribe of Dan. Dan had not yet fully settled into the reclaimed territory of Canaan. Manoah and his wife received a vision from the LORD that they would have a child who was to be especially dedicated to God.

At Ekron, archaeologists excavated a Philistine centre in 1981. Researchers found they could replicate the tools they found in digging. They were able to rebuild copies of ancient looms used by the Philistines, and have been able to weave cloth using the ancient Philistine methods.

Also discovered at Ekron were iron tools and weapons, pottery and kilns, and deities, some of which were among the idols detested by the Israelites. Scholars determined that the Philistines were sea people, who were traders around the Mediterranean, and probably originated from the Aegean, perhaps from Cyprus or Mycenae or both.

THE PHILISTINES

The Philistines were the leading people in a great invasion of Syria around 1175 B.C. in the reign of Egypt's Rameses III. Genesis 26 mocks the stupidity of the Philistines. The stories of Samson also contrast Israelite cleverness with Philistine ineptitude. The Philistines, part of the Semitic race, are described as uncircumcised. They were the only inhabitants in Palestine so described.

Exodus claims that Philistines were already in Palestine when the Israelites were leaving Egypt. Like the Hebrews, the Philistines took over the Semitic language of the country of their adoption. Living in the regions of the Aegean Sea, the Philistines reached Canaan and settled along the coastal plain. Soon they were in conflict with the Israelites. This conflict between the Philistines and Israelites lasted throughout the period of the Judges.

The principle base of settlement and power for the Philistines was a group of five towns near the coast: Gaza, Ashkelon, Ashdod, Ekron, and Gath. They organized under five "lords," each with his own city. By the mid-11th century BC they overwhelmed the Israelites by controlling the manufacture of iron tools and weapons. In 1050 BC they destroyed Shiloh, the Hebrew worship centre at the time, capturing the Ark of the Covenant.

During Saul's reign he checkmated Philistia. David subdued them though not eliminating them in the tenth century. Following Sennacherib's Assyrian invasion at the close of the eighth century BC they all but vanished from the records. Although they survived in their cities for 300 more years they eventually were absorbed by the conquering Assyrians.

SAMSON

Samson was the Judge with long hair. As long as his uncut hair grew he had tremendous strength. He fought the Philistines, then was betrayed to them by Delilah, who, having discovered his secret, cut his hair while he was asleep.

Samson was born a Danite. Dan, one of the 12 tribes of Israel, had not yet found a permanent home. Their semi-permanent camp was in the hill country, west of Jerusalem and near the coastal plain used by the Philistines.

Before his birth, Samson's parents dedicated him to God's service. They called him a Nazarite, a holy man so long as his hair went uncut. He abstained from strong drink, nor could he touch a human corpse! From early in his life, not only his parents, but the whole tribe felt Samson's abilities were God-given. He became a tribal leader. Samson judged Israel for 20 years.

Samson was attracted to women outside this tribe. He wed a Philistine woman, lost a reckless bet at his wedding party, killed 30 Philistines and stole their goods to pay off debts. Samson went back to camp without his bride!

Delilah, the final flirt of Samson's life, betrayed her man. She learned the secret of his strength and set about to cut his hair. With his strength gone, Samson was captured, blinded and enslaved by the Philistines.

Over time, Samson's hair grew long again. His strength returned. He was brought to the pagan Philistine temple at a time of celebration as an object of ridicule. In turn, the revitalized Samson was able to seize and collapse two main pillars of the temple. The roof fell upon the revellers, and Samson dying along with them.

Sadly, the great vision of Joshua, Moses, Joseph, Israel, Isaac and Abraham had lost a measure of its promise. Not only were the Israelites often subject to their powerful neighbours, but they often were subject to inter-nicene, inter-tribal fighting among themselves. At one point the entire tribe of Benjamin was almost decimated. People began to realize that they needed another Joshua to keep them in focus and to unite them in purpose and spiritual direction.

The people of Israel saw that the nations surrounding them were united by a monarch. They wanted to be seen as a nation also. Their call for a king of Israel slowly grew from a quiet whisper to a loud mantra. *"We want a King!* **We want a king!***"*

THE CONCEPT OF THEOCRACY

Initially, the Israelites looked to their Patriarchs as leaders, then to the lawgiver Moses, followed by the invader, Joshua, then the Judges and early prophets. As the Israelites watched other nations, they also coveted a monarchial-style nation for themselves. Israel may have elected Saul as king but he soon showed that he vacillated between melancholy and bravery.

When David became the apparent new ruler of Israel, he was blessed by the prophet Samuel as being God's anointed one. "Anointed One" is the term used to describe "Messiah." As we read the Bible, we quickly discover that in many of the sacred songs – the psalms – the king is regarded as a Messiah. Hence, when Jesus lived on the earth, he was also referred to as Messiah (or Christ, in Greek) and as the "Son of David."

The psalms which refer to Israel's king as YAWEH's messiahs are known to us as the "Royal Psalms." They are intended to remind all worshippers that Israel's king was divinely appointed. In turn, that meant Israel's king had divine responsibilities to be a representative priest on behalf of the people to God himself.

The anointed one enjoyed a privileged but severe responsibility. While his rule was guaranteed by YAHWEH, his work and life must always be understood to be under YHWH's divine control. Rewards and punishment alike were shared by messiah and people. The anointed one was blessed but so were the people. The messiah of God was punished but so were the people.

The Davidic kingdom was always to be the idealized monarchy because it was the first monarchy of a truly victorious and saving messiah. He united the nation as had no previous leader and extended the limits of the kingdom as had no other general. Moreover, as the prophet Samuel indicated, he was chosen for his spiritual leadership as much as for his valour. "God looks on the heart," said Samuel as he anointed David.

Out of the decimated tribe of Benjamin, the tribe almost obliterated from inter-tribal bickering, came one who seemed, at the time, to be everything the people wanted in their king. Little did the people know that for every strength he had to offer, he was matched with equal weaknesses. As we shall see in the next chapter, Benjamin's seed survived to produce Israel's first king, King Saul.

CHAPTER 7

CHARISMA AND KINGSHIP

As we noted in the previous chapter, following the Israelite reconquest of Canaan, led by the leader extraordinaire, Joshua, the people of Israel suffered from a paucity of national leadership. None of the judges of Israel ever earned national status, and none had the capacity to sustain, maintain or ascertain the combined needs of spiritual and political situations which Moses and Joshua were capable of solving.

Israel lacked a genuine charismatic leader. The Israelites took two steps forward and three backwards during the period of the "judges." No overall leader rose to the occasion.

The nation lacked unity and direction. The weakness was obvious; the people suffered too much as a result of the influence of their polytheistic, pagan neighbours. The cry went up, "We want a king!" Their choice was Saul, an impressive and dramatic young man, without equal among the Israelites. He offered security and protection against the Philistines and Canaanites.

Meanwhile God had chosen a different kind of leader, not a warrior like Joshua but a man of God's choosing to bring spiritual stability to the Israelites. His name was Samuel. The prophet Samuel was to provide spiritual leadership to his people while Saul was to provide Israel's military direction.

However, Saul's stature, of being a head taller than any others, did not translate into stable leadership. Soon another king needed to be anointed. Surprise! It would be a shepherd boy who grew up to defeat giants.

CHOOSING SAUL'S SUCCESSOR

Saul was Israel's first king. The decision to select a king stemmed from two sources. One was Israel's dissatisfaction with the ungodly priests appointed by the priest Eli. The other reason was that every neighbour nation had a king, and Israel wanted to be like them. God, through Samuel, warned the people that if the people wanted a king, they were also opting for warfare.

God's prophet Samuel anointed Saul as king of Israel and told him God had appointed him to look after his "inheritance," that is, the Israelites. The Israelites soon discovered that Saul possessed a manic depressive personality, ranging between a fearless drive to defeat his enemies, and cowering in fear because of them. Even when chosen king, Saul hid among the baggage while the people sought him in order to covenant with him. When Saul grew older he sank into melancholia, romanced with the occult, sought advice from mediums, and flew into rages of jealousy. It was apparent that Israel did not need such leadership. Samuel put it bluntly to the king: "Because you have rejected the word of the LORD, he has rejected you as king."

Even before Saul had died, Samuel was engaged by God to select another king. Saul's successor was not to be his offspring. Rather, God wanted a king to set an example both of bravery and righteousness. The choice of king was made by denoting character. The LORD said to Samuel, his prophet, "Do not consider his appearance or his height. The LORD does not look at the things man looks at. Man looks at the outward appearance, but the LORD looks at the heart."

God led the prophet Samuel to Bethlehem. All but one of the sons of Jesse were mustered before the prophet of God to see if he would choose one of them. The prophet dismissed each of them. Yet Samuel sensed that someone was missing.

"There is still the youngest. But he is tending the sheep," said Jesse. Samuel responded, "Send for him." David came and was anointed by the prophet of God. David would succeed Saul as king.

David was a king-in-waiting. Not one to challenge King Saul, he tried his best to co-operate with the king. Theirs was a bittersweet relationship, Saul at times promoting David's fame and at times fully prepared to slay the young Bethlehemite. Saul's son and David became the very closest of friends and the son, Jonathan, often warned David of intrigue against him from within Saul's court. For a while, David found it necessary to exile himself among the Philistines, and sometimes to become a pirate, raiding caravans or pagan cities to make a living. He and his guerilla group, found shelter in the hills of Judah and Philistia.

THE CAVE OF ADULLAM

One of the earliest stories we hear about King David, was that he was a lad who practised using the slingshot. Out on the hill slopes of Bethlehem, while guarding his father Jesse's sheep, he had time to set up targets, and perfect his aim. He used his honed skill to target wolves, foxes and jackals – even lions and bears – which had eyes for straying lambs and the sheep under David's charge.

Shooting with slingshot and stone must have been a mideastern pastime. One of the stories in the book of Judges tells us that Israel had a complete division of troops who were left-handed sharpshooters. Referring to these 700 soldiers, the Bible says: "Out of all the 26,000 men who draw the sword . . . 700 choice men were left-handed; each one could sling a stone at a hair and not miss."

No wonder, with all David's practice on the hills and in the valleys near Bethlehem, he was prepared to meet the Philistine giant, Goliath. He thought to himself, "He's so big I can't miss!"

In time, David found himself "on the outs" with Saul, the king of Israel. David found refuge in the Cave of Adullam, a cave somewhere in Philistine country.

He also gathered about him a small band of guerrillas who quietly and gradually were drawn to him. First his brothers joined him, the same brothers who made fun of him prior to his fight with Goliath. And then the castoffs of society began to trickle south and east to join David's raiding party.

The Bible says of them, "And every one who was in distress, and every one who was in debt, and every one who was discontent, gathered to him: and he became captain over them. Now there were about 400 men with him."

We say that "cream rises to the top." David was cream – definitely! In this case the genius of David was obvious to people. David had the stamp of leadership planted firmly on his person. If he would be the leader, these castoffs would follow him anywhere, no matter the danger.

David was a hill-and-crag guerrilla fighter, with the other amazing side of his life to compose, we believe, such a thing as the 23rd Psalm. He was tough, resilient, canny. He was brutal to enemies, but also had a marvellous conscience and sense of decency, as when he spared Saul's life. He cut a piece off Saul's garment to prove that he had been there and could have killed Saul. The weapons, landscapes and great

ABIGAIL AND DAVID'S WIVES

There lived in the vicinity of Hebron, a wealthy farmer named Nabal. His name may mean "fool." He had great herds of sheep, goats and camels. Nabal, along with other countrymen, enjoyed the protection offered by David and his men. The season arrived for sheep shearing. David felt that this was a propitious time to appeal to Nabal for some food and goods that might sustain his fighting men. So David sent men to the tent of Nabal and asked for these supplies. Nabal, celebrating the shearing harvest in a drunken stupor, denied this request and humiliated the men of David in front of those in his tent. They returned and told David of this incident. David decided to pay Nabal his just dues. He armed his men and took them to Nabal's camp.

Meanwhile, one of Nabal's servants hied off to tell Nabal's wife Abigail what had occurred and to forewarn her that David would not take this denial lightly. This strong, dynamic lady knew decidedly what to do.

She went to the kitchens and selected certain prize foods – baked items, figs, raisins, grapes, wine – and saw that all of this provender was loaded on the donkeys. She rushed away to meet David before he came to wreak havoc on Nabal. When they met, she entreated David with words such as these: "As the Lord liveth, the Lord hath withheld you from shedding blood."

To make a long story short, David was won over by this beautiful and talented Abigail.

The drug-witted Nabal, when told by Abigail, how close he came to losing all, suffered a fatal stroke. As in all good stories, David married Abigail. He knew a smart woman when he saw one.

distances of those times make for dramatic viewing. What organizational ability to get the job done and to craft a nation! David was warrior, friend to Jonathan, leader and organizer, lover, musician and poet.

David was in close touch with his God, but at times betrayed that relationship by the vilest of actions. He was equal to the task required of a king, and set out to build the nation. At first he was wildly popular, largely because of his reputation as a soldier, especially against the Philistines, but he was also respected for the way in which he refused to undermine the rule of King Saul, whom he respected.

DAVID AND THE JEBUSITES

One of David's early assignments was to take the land which was occupied by the Jebusites. The Jebusite believed that their stronghold of Jebus was invincible, able to be defended by the "blind and the lame," as the Jebusites yelled at David's army from the safety of Jebusite ramparts. But David's soldiers knew better. They found a weakness in the defence of Jebus, sent soldiers into the city by way of the watershaft and conquered the city.

Jebus was adjacent to where Abraham met Melchizedek, and was nearby where Abraham considered offering Isaac as a sacrifice. Jebus became Jerusalem, and with that change from Jebusite occupation, also became the central city of the united monarchy which David established.

Excavating at what is now part of the hill leading into the temple area, archaeologists, led by Yigal Shilo, have uncovered the city which was once David's and which was the capital of Judah until destroyed by the Babylonians in and around 586 B.C.

David earned renown but had clay feet. All biblical personnae have darks sides! More is known of David's dark side in the latter years of his rule. He was not a good father. He arranged the death of a loyal soldier, Uriah, in order to marry his widow whom he had impregnated.

He lost touch with the people he governed. By his disobedience of God he was not permitted to build the great Temple he envisaged, very much like Moses, through his disobedience of God's command, was punished by not being allowed into the promised land.

Yet Jesus did not think it beneath him to be called "The Son of David." For apart from the dark nature revealed about him in the Bible, David was a lover of God, conscious of his higher sovereignty, and fully aware that he was anointed by God for an important work.

If David was not to build a Temple to the LORD, then his son Solomon would. Solomon was anointed king, at the Spring of Gihon, the very place where David's soldiers launched their attack on the city of Jebus.

Solomon soon established his credentials with the people. He undertook the task of preparing to build the Temple, the first permanent house of God of the Israelite nation. It surely would unite Israel in a common work, a common worship and a common wealth. It also would unite them in a common debt. The Temple was extravagant in beauty and in price.

Solomon also undertook other expansions. One was in trade, another in agriculture. Yet another was in mining. In the southern reaches of Solomon's kingdom, at Timnah near Eilat, are remnants of copper mining from earlier Egyptian settlements and by Solomon. He cemented relationships with neighbouring nations by marrying foreign wives. Neither nation nor people benefitted from that manoeuvre.

THE TEMPLE OF SOLOMON

The people and especially the king wanted to dismiss the Tabernacle and replace it with a Temple. It would be a place where God allowed his Name to reside.

David never did built the Temple: that honour went to his son Solomon whose reign lasted from 970 to 930 BC. It may have looked impressive to a people nearby. Solomon's Temple was small, merely 30 meters long and 15 meters high. Built on the area of the same great rock used by David to offer a sacrifice, the Temple was quarried from stone nearby and cedar wood imported from Lebanon.

The king's Red Sea copper mines paid for skilled Phoenician workmen and the fine wood, gold and bronze. Solomon taxed the people and trader spice caravans for Temple decorations. Sadly, Solomon's Temple met an unkind fate in 586 BC as Jews began Babylonian captivity. A second Temple was built at the end of the exile. Herod the Great enlarged it. Herod's version of the Second Temple was magnificent building after the Roman style. It perched like a wonderful white and gold jewel atop the Temple Mount.

The Temple was a series of courtyards surrounding a central building. The largest section was the Court of the Gentiles, open to all. Up a flight of stairs, one entered by a series of gates the Court of Women, off-limits to non-Jews.

The Court of Israel was reserved for men only. Nearby, the Court of Priests had areas for sacrifices to be offered on a stone altars. The last space was the Holy of Holies. The Temple housed the Ark of the Covenant moved from a tent. In Herod's Temple it was an empty, dark room with a veil covering the entrance. No one entered this space except the high priest and that only once a year.

SOLOMON'S MINES

In Deuteronomy, Moses promised the Children of Israel that when they entered their Promised Land, they would – among other things – have a land where bread would "not be scarce." Moses told them, "You will lack nothing. [It is] a land where rocks are iron and you can dig copper out of the hills."

This was not an unmerited boast. As far back as the fourth millennium BC, tribes in the area of Timnah near the Red Sea collected surface copper. Then, they began to mine beneath the surface. The Timnah mines, dubbed "Solomon's Mines," appear to be the first shaft-and-gallery mines ever discovered.

Miners, slaves of the Egyptians, extracted copper by mixing it with iron and oxide ore. The smelters were primitive furnaces in pit form, dug in the ground. By using bellows, together with the unique winds in the Timnah region, the miners raised the temperatures of the furnace to 1,240 degrees. This produced a mass slag containing drops of copper which manually were extracted from the slag. In turn, this produced copper objects. When combined with tin, the copper made bronze, the standard armament until just before King Solomon's reign.

The Egyptian New Kingdom turned these early, more primitive mining and smelting projects into permanent, well-organized camps. They served the pharaohs very well.

Ore was crushed in a central area on a platform, and side rooms and storage pits were kept to one side of the central ore-crushing area. The Egyptian smelting-furnace produced a copper ingot. Slag from the melting furnace was tapped into a slag pit at the front of the furnace and the ingot removed from its bottom.

The Egyptians ensured that proper religious niceties were observed by their provision of temples and worship centres which they constructed, even engaging an "industrial chaplain" and his accommodation. This was a forerunner of pastor and manse! It was for their Semite workers.

Solomon also expanded his larger enterprises by establishing contracts and linkages with foreign powers. Well known is his visit from the Queen of Sheba, who brought Solomon many gifts, but with her skills in flattery, left with more than she brought.

As noted, some of Solomon's alliances were made by intermarriage with the daughters of foreign rulers. These were considered political tokens. But with Solomon's political marriages, came also the larger expenses of state, and more imprudently, the religious inclinations of the monarch's domestic family. Shrines for the wives of Solomon dotted the horizon on what was called the Mount of Evil Counsel, facing towards the Great Temple he had established as the religious centre of his kingdom.

Today we have some hint at the various religious practices of groups which were in vogue during the years of David and Solomon. Some of these are in evidence at the place dubbed "Solomon's Pillars."

THE PILLARS OF SOLOMON

Just north of Eilat are natural rock formations of considerable beauty. Known now as "Solomon's Pillars," these sandstone hills honour the fact that King Solomon used the area widely both as a trading and shipping centre, and also as a source of copper mining, Geologists suggest that these hills were created more than 235 million years ago, during the Palaeozoic Period.

Nearby are sandstone arches which, swept by wind erosion, have created beautiful arches and dynamic rock formations. Alongside some rock faces, in the crevices, ancient artists carved chariot drawings.

Three or four hundred years prior to Solomon's reign, Egyptians settled in the area. First and foremost to any ancient civilization or community was its assurance that their divinities guarded them, to protect them from evil and potential enemies. Deities ensured each project's success. Hence the Hathor Temple in the place, built by Egyptian miners. It became the chief worship centre for the entire area.

Hathor was an Egyptian goddess, also known as the "joy goddess." In this region she was venerated as the Mistress of the Turquoises, perhaps because so much precious turquoise stone – we know it as malachite stone – was uncovered as a byproduct of copper mining in the region.

Hathor enjoyed several aliases. At Thebes, upstream in the Nile, Hathor was associated with Isis, guardian of the necropolis. In translation to the Greek religions, she was identified with Aphrodite, hence her powers of dancing and love. She was represented as a cow, and also in human form with cow's ears, or head or horns. Sometimes she is depicted with cow's ears and the solar disc between her horns.

The fertility cult of Hathor, and all lewdness that accompanied it, thrived for a while near the Solomon's Pillars. Later it became a Midianite centre of worship. By the end of Solomon's reign it ceased to function altogether.

This particular Midianite shrine may have ceased to function *during* Solomon's reign. But one negative inheritance Solomon gave to his descendants was the bent to worship foreign gods in order to protect the political integrity of his nation. That was not what God intended for his children of Israel, as we shall see in the next chapter.

CHAPTER 8

INSTRUCTION BY PROPHESY

In the previous chapter we noted, the people of Israel, led by Joshua as both strategist and spiritual leader, brought the people of Israel from their wilderness wanderings into the promised land. Joshua's death left a political and spiritual vacuum in the land. Judges periodically appeared, helter-skelter. They offered sporadic leadership in localized areas. Pagan neighbours influenced the beliefs of the new generation of Israelites. It should have been the other way around. God told Abraham that his offspring would be a "blessing" to the nations.

The Israelites also seemed more interested in addressing their lack of political leadership than their spiritual decline. However, God did not forsake his errant people. From the time of the Judges until after the exile to Babylon, God raised up among them spiritual spokespersons to give leadership to meet the needs of the people. These were the prophets.

ROLE OF THE PROPHETS

Moses has been called a prophet but the prophets whom God provided to the people of Israel were different in many ways from Moses' role. Most of the prophets surfaced after the Judges, and continued until John the Baptist arrived at his baptismal site in Jordan.

The word "prophet" derives from the Greek *pro-phetes*, "one who speaks on behalf of another, a herald and announcer." This in turn comes from the Hebrew word *nabi*, "one who is called." And so a prophet is one who is called by God to speak not his own words but the words of God himself.

Throughout history God has called on prophets to speak to his chosen people, particularly at times when their lives had moved away from their keeping of commandments. God wanted to call them back to a righteous way of living – a "walk" (*halakah*) with the Almighty. The prophet's message was seldom silenced. Some prophets were muted, even murdered.

The early prophets sought to discover God's will for his people at specific times. Their focus was on Israel's disobedience to the Law given by God to Moses.

Later prophets were known more as literary people of God. Their proclamations and teachings helped in the formation of Judaism. They brought the Israelites to a new, more profound understanding of God, especially in such important areas as God's covenants through Abraham, Moses and David.

Prophets saw themselves as spokespersons for God. They spoke out against evil and sin. They didn't worry about the consequences. They spoke up for the poor and downtrodden. They were the voice of the voiceless.

Someone said that a prophet is one who "comforted the afflicted, and afflicted the comfortable."

Samuel was the first of these major prophets. His name sounds like the Hebrew, "Heard by the LORD." Samuel anointed two kings, Saul and then David. He had considerable influence on the political events of his nation, as "Chaplain to the Court."

Two other prophets, whose activities are recorded in the books of Samuel, Kings and Chronicles, are the itinerant prophets Elijah and Elisha. Both were of equal spiritual strength and generally in accord with one another.

SAMUEL — PROPHET OF RENEWAL

Centuries ago, at Shiloh, a woman stood in the centre for worship and quietly prayed for a man child. If God should honour her prayer, Hannah would offer the child for the LORD's service. The priest, observing the lips of Hannah moving with no uttered sound, criticized this poor childless mother as being drunk with wine.

God answered the prayers of Hannah and she brought her son Samuel ("Asked of God") to the shrine and entrusted him to Eli's care. Samuel soon saw that in his mentor's home difficulties abounded. His two sons were problem children. They would have a natural right to succeed their father but were unfit to priest. Samuel lived in the high priest's residence.

One night as Samuel slept on his pallet he woke to hear his name. Was Eli calling him? He wasn't. Hardly had Samuel fallen asleep a second time when he heard his name again, and once more Samuel went to his master and asked him if there was need of him. Again, Eli told the boy to go to bed. At the third experience of this, Eli, wise enough to comprehend the ways of the Lord, told Samuel to return to his bed, and should he again hear his name called, to answer: "Speak, Lord, for your servant hears." This he did.

The LORD God told Samuel of the failure of the sons of Eli the priest and that he, Samuel, was chosen to be the spiritual leader for these people rather than Eli's sons. God's call could not be clearer to the child Samuel. God heard a mother's prayer, set the tone for a child to obey his call, and taught Eli to be attentive. God's call was never uncertain to Samuel from that moment on. The prophet arrived on God's timetable at a time the Israelites sorely needed him.

Elijah preceded Elisha and was his mentor. But as we shall see, being a prophet was no easy task. It was dangerous, daunting and draining.

EVENTS AT MT. CARMEL

Mount Carmel near present-day Haifa hosted a contest between the prophet Elijah and 400 priests of Baal, the fertility deity worshipped by pagans. Elijah on God's side faced the 400 on Baal's side.

Elijah was sent by God, partly, to confront those who bowed down to Baal. His task was formidable. In part, Elijah's task was to confront Israel's King Ahab about attaching himself to his wife Jezebel's faithlessness. She came from a neighbouring nation whose people practised lewd and ungodly religious rites. Jezebel, through her charm and lies, gradually led Ahab's people away from the worship of Israel's God to adopt service to Baal.

Crowds gathered atop Carmel near Baal's altar to witness the contest between Elijah and Baal's 400 priests. Would Jehovah or Baal win this battle for the souls of Israel?

An ox was slaughtered and its carcass spread out on an altar. But no fire was lit. Priests called on Baal to light the fire. They screamed, danced, cut themselves in a frenzy. But nothing happened. Elijah challenged them. "Shout louder, maybe he is asleep or gone off to the toilet." As sunset came, Baal's priests gave way to Elijah. He rebuilt the altar fit for worshipping Jehovah. He slew an ox and laid it out on the altar. Water from the Kishom stream was then poured over the ox until it filled a ditch around the altar.

The crowds and the priests waited. Elijah called on Jehovah, his God. Fire fell from heaven, consuming the sacrifice. Elijah shouted to the people. "If Baal is God then follow him. If Jehovah is God follow him." The people responded, "The Lord is God. The Lord is God." The priests of Baal were slaughtered. Elijah then proceeded to pray for rain.

Elijah, worn out in victory, rushed off to King Ahab to tell him that the drought and famine were over. Jezebel, however, terrified Elijah. He fled her in fear. While strong in the Lord, he was still a weak and frightened man. He fled to the south and at the place where God gave the Law to Moses, the Lord ministered to and refreshed him

By the time Elijah and Elisha ministered to the offspring of Israel, the nation once united by David and Solomon had divided into two portions, known in the north as Israel and in the south as Judah. Judah consisted of two tribal units, the tribe of Judah and the tribe of Benjamin. The term "Jews" means descendants of Judah.

Too soon the dire predictions of these prophets came true. First the northern kingdom, Israel – the ten northern tribes – were removed by the Assyrians. They ceased to exist as pure tribal groupings, and are still referred to as the "ten lost tribes."

A century and a half later, the southern kingdom, Judah, collapsed, its citizens led in chains to Babylon. The book of Isaiah predicted both the demise of Judah and later its reconstruction and hope.

In spite of their decline as nations, north and south, the Jews especially were given hope, not only for a political entitlement, but for a spiritual destiny. Even in exile God was engaging his people through his ministers, the prophets. Ezekiel was a captive taken to Babylon in the first wave of deportees. He was a priest to whom God assigned the additional role of prophet.

SOME MINOR PROPHETS

Some of God's prophets, such as Amos, ministered in both nations – to Israel in the north and Judah in the south. He was a fruit and fig farmer, a godly layman from Tekoa in Judah. God gave Amos a divinely-sent message to be delivered to the northern kingdom. Leaving his farming to others, he ventured north and set out for the northern kingdom's capital, Samaria. His role was to speak about (a) justice (tsedakah) for all and; (b) for Samaria's integrity in divine worship experiences. Tsedakah means both justice and righteousness.

Micah was a southerner, a prophet in his own country, but not necessarily received well. Unlike Amos, Micah brought God's serious word to the people of Judah, imploring them to worship God with integrity and to practise the standard of morality and justice that God expected from the people with whom he had covenanted. He spoke urgently about repentance.

The prophet Hosea could have sung the spiritual, "Nobody knows the troubles I've seen," throughout his ministry. He married a wayward harlot. His lot was to be a living parable of God's love for his people. In that parable he acted out how God, the true lover, was injured time and again by the adulterous behaviour of his spouse, Israel, whom he loved dearly.

Jeremiah, a most reticent servant of God, prophesied the collapse of Judah. Like Hosea he was a reluctant prophet who endured severe hardships as he acted out the parable of Judah in slavery. Jeremiah's text is long but written with intensity and courage. When Jerusalem destructed, Jeremiah was heard from no more.

ISAIAH: THE MAKING OF A PROPHET

Isaiah was a court preacher in Jerusalem during the eighth century BC. His prophetic writings are well-known and loved by Jews and Christians today. They speak of God's love for his people. They speak also of God's displeasure with a sinful nation. Isaiah's writing contains many warnings of future events.

Without mentioning "Jesus" directly, Isaiah spoke eloquently of the Saviour who was to come. It mentions the Suffering Servant's work and pictures him as God's pained and ridiculed man who one day would be despised and rejected. Isaiah foretold the coming of the Saviour. Then and in the future? His words speak of a God who is awesome and powerful, yet gentle and loving. Isaiah speaks metaphorically of the man Jesus, who was God.

At worship one day, Isaiah received a special call and commission from God. God told him he would be a prophet of God, one who would speak and act as God's spokesperson to his people. Isaiah was a gifted orator. His words were beautiful pieces of poetry evoking images of a loving God who cared about his people.

Very little is known of Isaiah except that his faith must have been deep and strong. His words have moved many a Jew and Christian to repent and return to God. Often his words were difficult to interpret. Sometimes only a few people in high places understood his meanings.

Isaiah's announcements were spoken in the style of other prophets, like Daniel, whose task was to speak about times "yet to come." His work is divided at the 40th chapter with what may be a prophecy during Judah's exile, and Judah's imminent return. Certainly the mood of his prophecy changes abruptly after chapter 39.

EZEKIEL: PRIEST, PROPHET, PREACHER

Ezekiel was a young man about age 20 when he was taken, along with his parents, into Babylonian exile. During this period in exile God called on him to prophesy. His was a daunting task for so young a man, exiled from his homeland. The year was around 597 – 586 BC.

Ezekiel's prophetic role was as a visionary. His people, although exiled, were able to live their lives much the same as usual. They prospered, owned homes, carried out business ventures just as if they had back at home.

Things were not as smooth for Ezekiel. God had rugged plans for him. God allowed him to experience a sense of profound loss. Later, he could relate that loss to God's experience with his people and their relationship with God. Ezekiel lost his wife, very dear to him, the "apple of his eye." Later, he shared his experience of devastating loss like Jerusalem's complete destruction.

Did Ezekiel suffer from seizures? Could these have been the times when God spoke to him through visions? His prophecies were certainly filled with imagery not the result of everyday experiences. God told him do some strange things. Ezekiel was to lay on his side for 390 days and then for a further 40 days on the other side (4:6). These numbers represented the years of guilt associated with Israel and Judah.

On another occasion, he removed some hairs from his head and beard. Part of these he burned. Another part he struck with his sword while yet another he scattered to the winds. This symbolized how the people would be decimated so that only a small remnant would remain.

HAGGAI : THE TEMPLE BUILDER

Haggai identifies himself in the book by his name as "Haggai the prophet." He may not have been old when he assumed his prophetic office.

His special responsibility was to restore the house of God to the city rebuilt during the time of Nehemiah and Ezra. As energetic and enthusiastic as was Nehemiah in rebuilding the walls, God asked Haggai to create a special hunger and desire for rebuilding the Temple. His messages to the people probably commenced in the year 520 BC. Rebuilding saw several delays, some caused by the Samaritans who had scant respect for the Temple.

Returning immigrants, limited their spiritual exercises to building an altar for their burnt offerings. For 16 years the Temple's rebuilding stalled. Peripheral matters governed spiritual life, all with good purpose, but not all for rebuilding of the House of God. Money-making schemes sometimes interfered with the real work of God. What else is new?

Against this indifference and apathy that Jerusalem's citizens showed about the House of God, Haggai sprang to action. He spoke out against the programs and policies that interfered with this rebuilding. His preaching was of a plain style. He repeated himself (for good reason?). The intensity of his preaching and the vigour of his speech, gained the hearing of the people. They began to rebuild the Temple.

In chapter two of the Book of Haggai, one discovers this truth: "Holiness is not contagious, but unholiness is." Profoundly earnest, plain prophet Haggai got the ear of God's people and they set out to build the House of the Lord.

When they returned from exile, the Jews were not yet deprived of God's spiritual leaders, the prophets. Haggai, whose tomb is venerated on the Mount of Olives, engaged the Jews in spiritual introspection to incite them to godliness and purity.

Haggai, along with the exiled Jewish families who returned to Judah, was part and parcel of the rebuilding process. Nehemiah was the strategist who persuaded the ruler of Persia to let the Jews return and to rebuild Jerusalem's city walls. Nehemiah also set about to rebuild the shattered spiritual life of Jerusalem, and introduced reforms which brought the people back to the faith handed down to them through Moses. Another leader, Ezra, saw that the Temple was properly rebuilt. But renewed energy also can dissipate and so another prophet, Malachi, reminded the Jews that their Temple must never be taken for granted. It was indeed the house of the LORD.

Last, but certainly not least of the prophets, was Zechariah. He joined God's heralds who taught God's word for his people following the return of the Jews to Jerusalem. His was another voice to help create the vision of a Messianic age, and a servant of the LORD's who was to be God's ultimate prophet and leader for his people.

ZECHARIAH

Zechariah, a contemporary of Haggai, ministered to the Jews who were returning from Babylon. He began his work during the reign of Darius. His name means, "The LORD remembers." His father was a priest and much of his prophecy concerns the high priesthood of Judah.

He began his written prophecy with a call for Judah

MALACHI: MESSENGER TO THE BORED

The excitement of renewal days passed and God's people became apathetic, indifferent, diffident and bored to death with spirituality. They liked the form of religion, however. People like tradition! That is why God called Malachi to address this need of the people.

First, he spoke to those recently returned from exile, who had seen Jerusalem rebuilt both in walls and with Temple, but now had become "ho-hum" about it all. Judah required a new call to repentance. Malachi made a powerful, passionate, pleading appeal to the people. He said that if they really knew the promises of God, they truly would repent.

Malachi told Judah that Judah had been cheating God of his percentage of dues. "Bring ye all the tithes into the storehouse, that there may be meat in mine house; and prove me now herewith, saith the Lord of Hosts, if I will not open you the windows of heaven, and pour you out a blessing, that there shall not be room enough to receive it!"

Then he proceeded to tell of God's justice for those who cheat him: "Behold, he shall come, saith the Lord of Hosts; but who may abide the day of his coming?"

to repent of its sins. He reviewed Jewish history's bad track record in this moral department. Much of his work, however was of restoration and promise for Jewish people. He did this by advancing several visions of the future, both of God's wrath on sin, and victory for those who walked in God's ways. In a sense, like Daniel's prophecy, he had adopted an apocalyptic style to get across God's messages. So while he predicted great harm, he anticipated great hope for God's people. He looked for a renewed Judah. All the world would look to Judah's God for peace and security. All would keep the Sabbath as directed and all would enjoy the great feast days as directed in the Torah.

Zechariah gave voice and vision to the Messiah who would come in humility, but reign as king. Read carefully and one will see Jesus in his words.

Of Nehemiah and Ezra we shall read more in the next chapter. We shall also look at the events which led to the fall of the northern kingdom, Israel, and see how the Jews preserved their identity and renewed their spirituality while they were exiled in Babylon.

CHAPTER 9

DIVIDE AND BE CONQUERED

In the previous chapter we saw how the LORD raised up voices of instruction to match the political leadership of the people of Israel and to guide the people in God's precepts. They were called prophets. After the one nation under David, then Solomon, split into two parts – Israel and Judah – the prophets continued to address the spirituality of each of the two kingdoms. In each case, their message was similar and it consisted of two emphases. One was justice, the other godliness.

The northern kingdom, Israel, was the larger of the two divisions. It was also first to collapse. It reached its zenith a hundred years after Solomon, plateaued for a half-century, and then gradually fell into decline.

The capital of the northern kingdom was Samaria. Its name derived from Shemer, the man from whom King Omri bought the land to build his capital. The name Samaritan, however, was only attached to people who intermarried with settlers who came from Assyria and other states.

That followed 721 BC, when the northern kingdom called Israel was subjugated by Sargon II of Assyria. Most of the inhabitants of the northern kingdom were taken away to Assyria.

Once there, they assimilated with the Assyrian population. This group which left in the northern kingdom exodus is sometimes referred to as "the ten lost tribes." The ten lost tribes were not really lost; they knew exactly where they were. A few exiles returned in later years.

SEBASTE / SAMARIA

After Solomon's death, the single, united kingdom split in two. Rehoboam, Solomon's son, could not hold the united kingdom together. He was left with the south, Judah, its capital, Jerusalem.

The northern section, Israel, chose Jeroboam as king. When Omri usurped the northern throne 150 years later, he established a royal capital in the very midst of the northern country. Some called Israel, "Omriland." Omri chose Samaria as his capital. Located on high ground, close to the roads leading to Phoenicia, Galilee and Esdraelon, like Megiddo to the northwest, its location was strategic, both in war and peace. It seemed impregnable. King after king, for a 150 years held it. It controlled the trade routes, allowing the tax levying city to grow rich. Omri's military skill and his negotiating ability kept Israel at peace with its neighbours. Omri died after a reign of 12 years,

Skilled archaeological excavation in the first half of the 20th century revealed the wonder of the city. Central on top of the hill were the royal quarters. The palace was at least two stories high. King Ahaziah, successor to his father Ahab and grandfather Omri, fell from the balcony and later died. The royal area was surrounded by a strong wall built of cut and fitted rock behind which Ahab built a temple to Baal. Ahab married Jezebel, a daughter of the High Priest king of Tyre. She ardently worshipped Baal propagating that faith throughout the northern kingdom.

In the midst of it all, the prophet Elisha anointed Jehu king of Israel. In 721 BC the Assyrians captured Samaria, and burned much of it.

WHO ARE THE SAMARITANS?

Mount Gerizim was the geographical location where Samaritans worshipped God. They eschewed Jerusalem because it was David's city and they did not like David.

About 722 BC, the Assyrian King Sargon captivated thousands of the Jews and force-marched them to Assyria. As immigrants replaced the exiles, they inter-married remaining largely peasant class Israelites. This severed all Hebrew standards of racial purity. Throughout history these people of mixed ancestry offered to help the Jews on their return from a Babylonian exile with aid to rebuild Jerusalem's Temple. Jews rebuffed this offer. The people now known as Samaritans, built their own temple on Mount Gerizim.

Samaritans themselves describe their lineage and background in a somewhat different manner. They argue that they were a people who remained pure. They claim that the priest Eli seduced the people into building a shrine at Shiloh, when it ought to have been at Gerizim.

The Samaritans have had a long and difficult history of persecution. They have suffered much during their history. Only a small community of Samaritans exist today, largely in the troubled city of Nablus. They number less than 400.

How do they differ in terms of their religious customs as from the Jews? Not much! They observe the Sabbath, the sacred feasts, circumcision, and the conviction that a Messiah or a Restorer will yet come. Their faith is regulated by the words of the Pentateuch. Yet it is Mount Gerizim, not Jerusalem, that they still consider sacrosanct, the true abode of God on earth. They believe their priesthood lineage has descended directly from Aaron, the brother of Moses.

By the time the northern kingdom known as Israel had collapsed, the southern kingdom known as Judah was in rapid decline. At the same time, the nations of Assyria and Babylonia were in political ascendency.

Jerusalem, capital of Judah, was constantly threatened from without by various nations flexing military muscles: Egypt, Assyria, Babylon, Chaldea, Persia. The inhabitants of Judah also were in spiritual decline as the testimony of many of their prophets will attest. From time to time Judah's kings exhibited a conscience but more often than not, the record in the Bible states of a ruler, that "he did evil in the sight of the LORD!"

One of Hezekiah's plans to elude Sennacherib was to create a safe and adequate water supply for his city in case of siege. Still intact, after restoration earlier in the last century, is Hezekiah's Tunnel which brought the water supply through the hill, to the Pool of Siloam. This 570 meter snake-like tunnel was not long, but it would have prolonged the ability of Jerusalemites to withstand the siege of Sennacherib. Hurrying to forestall the apparent invasion, the tunnellers began their excavations at each end, and met in the centre, with only a half-meter inaccuracy. It was an engineering marvel.

CHANGES DURING EXILE

Jerusalem did fall – 15 years later. In the year 586 BC the city was burned by Nebuchadnezzar of Babylon. The people were led away in chains, and their city of Jerusalem, with its beautiful Temple built by Solomon four centuries earlier, was left in ruins.

The exile of the Jews in Babylon lasted 70 years.

SENNACHERIB

Twenty-seven centuries ago, Sennacherib ruled Assyria and Babylonia. Hezekiah was king of Judah, his capital, Jerusalem. Judah's king became a part of the general refusal of area kings to pay increased tributes to Assyria. Sennacherib marched his great army south around the fertile crescent, and soon controlled no less than 46 cities. He paused outside Jerusalem, demanded a ransom and received it. Hezekiah sent the Temple's wealth and his private riches as tribute. Sennacherib then demanded that the city surrender. Hezekiah balked. Encouraged by the prophet Isaiah, he asked God for deliverance.

Somewhat mysteriously, Sennacherib did withdraw with his armies, perhaps encouraged by rumours of rebellion in Babylon. Returning home and onward to Babylon, the rebellion was crushed, and thousands of the rebels were sent into exile, while Sennacherib's son Ashur-nadin-shumi was made king.

The conquered kingdoms of the south remained quiet and continued paying tribute. The Elamites, a nation to the east of Babylon, were a thorn in the flesh to Sennacherib who moved against its cities, won victories, and because of an extended supply line suffered some defeats. The outcome was rather indefinite. In retreat Sennacherib suffered an indefinite defeat near Babylon.

Two years later Sennacherib returned, conquered and razed the city of Babylon, even causing the ruins to be flooded by the river Euphrates.

His conquest was achieved. His two sons murdered him in 681 BC. Neither succeeded him.

While it began as a hideous ordeal and humiliation, the exile served somewhat the same purpose for the Jews as the wilderness did for the children of Israel. Deprived of political aspirations and shut out of governmental responsibility they once again started to become a community. They learned mathematics, science, and the arts. And most important they learned about books and organization. Deprived of the Temple they found substitute ways of enlarging their faith. When they had learned these things, God raised up a new leader – Nehemiah, master administrator. He was a courtesan in the service of Cyrus, King of Persia. Cyrus was a somewhat enlightened despot whose policy was to give considerable freedom to the communities he had conquered.

At the opportune moment, Nehemiah asked if he could go to the land of his fathers to rebuild the walls of Jerusalem. Cyrus co-operated. He even returned the treasures from the Temple which Nebuchadnezzar had looted. Ezra was Nehemiah's counterpart in this endeavour. Ezra seized upon the new insights into faith and life which the Jews had learned in far-off Babylon. Ezra was both a priest and a scribe.

"Scribe" is the operational word here, for the scribe was a new breed of religious leader, born out of the religious adjustments which were made by Jews in exile. He was a student of the Torah and as such became an interpreter of God's law. Ezra re-established genuine religious fervour in the rebuilt Jerusalem.

Jerusalem's walls were rebuilt, not without much harassment – by some whose political influence was reduced by Nehemiah's new role in leadership. Just as important in the rebuilding of the city is the rebuilding of a Jewish society which was the ministry of both Nehemiah and Ezra.

NEHEMIAH

Nehemiah, who lived during the fifth century BC, had, as his primary goal, the establishment and protection of a pure Jewish state.

He was appointed Governor of the newly re-created state of Judah by the King of Persia. Nehemiah served him as a court official. He quickly re-built the walls of Jerusalem, enacted laws to stamp out the lax attitude towards the law, and gradually re-established a pure, Judaic population.

Nehemiah knew that inter-marriage between Jews and foreigners meant that the family structure was being disrupted. No longer were the ways of the "chosen people" and their Torah being taught by parents, especially mothers, to their children. Judaism was in grave danger of being watered down, even destroyed.

Nehemiah enacted some tough laws. He cancelled all debts for the poor, giving them a new start. He broke up mixed marriages, stopping the tide that threatened to destroy the purity of the Jewish race.

He organized the lives of the Jewish community in Judah, making a covenant with the people to separate themselves from foreign nations. To accomplish this, he re-built the walls of Jerusalem in just 52 days, despite attacks from neighbouring provinces. Finally, Nehemiah re-established the marriage laws and Sabbath observance.

Nehemiah's task was to preserve and renew the Jewish faith, laws and culture. Not to have done so, was to risk having God's chosen people become impure, even lost. His role of prophet was not so much to warn of the dangers facing God's people, but to be given the authority and power to change things.

EZRA

The story of Ezra is set during the rule of Artaxerxes. In 539 BC Babylon was captured by King Cyrus of Persia. A year later he issued a decree permitting the Jews who had been deported to Babylon, to return to their homeland and rebuild it. Approximately 40,000 returned. The Temple was restored on its original site in Jerusalem. Ezra resolved to go to Jerusalem himself to inspect conditions there and reform the religious life of the returnees. He received official authorization from King Cyrus.

On his arrival in Jerusalem, Ezra set about restoring strict religious observance and reviewed the national identity of the people who had been weakened. He ordered all men from Jerusalem and surrounding area to assemble and hear his stern announcement. Many had married foreign women. All were compelled to separate themselves from their wives of foreign origin. Divorce proceedings lasted two months.

Ezra occupied a prominent place in later Jewish tradition. He dictated 94 books to replace those which had been lost in exile. Twenty-four of these are canonical books which were made public. The remaining 70 were kept secret for "the wise." Ezra became the preserver of the religious tradition from its earlier stages.

He read the codified scriptures which he had brought from Babylon. Because of reading and study of the Law, the thanksgiving Festival of Succoth was revived. The harvest Festival of Succoth commemorated the time when Israelite ancestors were led out of Egypt by Moses.

Ezra consolidated both the religious and legal code of the small Jewish community. He laid the foundation for Judaism to develop as a creed and way of life.

Beginning with the exile, the Jews made accommodations in their religious activities and observances. Without a Temple in exile, and deprived of opportunities to practise their traditional religious observances, such as their three-times-a-year visit to the temple in Jerusalem, they created synagogues where scribes could teach the law.

Gradually, the scribes and the emerging rabbinical group were offering a book-centred faith, a substitute accommodation when the Temple observances were not possible. With the return to Judah, and even though the Temple was rebuilt, the returning exiles brought the idea of synagogues with them. Instead of diminishing because of the return to priestly functions, the rabbinical methods increased and institutionalized themselves. In fact, the synagogues also provided a school system for Jewish children.

Upon Alexander's death, four of his generals carved up the known world for their individual empires. One to inherit a section of it was a sinister figure named Antiochus Epiphanes. He not only imposed his Greek religion on the people of Judah but desecrated the Temple of God by offering swine's flesh on the Temple's main altar. It was an "abomination of desolation" as we shall see in the next chapter of this book.

WHAT IS A SYNAGOGUE?

A synagogue is a gathering of people who assemble to study and to pray, and to learn about the word of God. Sometimes synagogue is confused with a building. It is both, like church is both people and meeting place.

Unlike the Temple no sacrifice is offered. It has no altar. One of the males in the synagogue will read the passage of the day and may, or someone else, explain its implication. This is not the work of a priest but a teacher. A cabinet (the Ark) is at the front and holds the one indispensable object – the Torah – the scroll on which was written the commandments by which Jews are to live their lives. The synagogue is a gathering place where they came to learn and to understand really what it was that God wanted them to do with their lives.

The first synagogues were not fixed places, but portable sanctuaries which could be set up wherever a congregation of ten male family heads could gather. As the Jewish people gradually ceased to become nomadic and settled in towns and cities, these meeting places became permanent structures.

Later, Rabbis offered prayer within the synagogues, carrying on the covenantal dialogue of men speaking and God listening. Learning / teaching, however, is always its primary function. The Jewish synagogue (Greek word, by the way) influenced early Christian worship,

CHAPTER 10

DEFYING DESOLATION

In the previous chapter we noted how the Jewish exiles returned from their unwanted sojourn in Babylon. When they re-established their homeland and their faith activities they were like people reborn. The biblical accounts of Ezra and Nehemiah cannot mask the freshness and vitality of their faith and life.

Nonetheless, the rise of Alexander the Great and his empire, and subsequently the Romans, changed daily life for every Jew. Between Alexander's invasions and the rise of the Roman empire, the Seleucid general Antiochus Epiphanes made life unbearable for the Jews.

ANTIOCHUS EPIPHANES

The Bible makes no direct mention of Antiochus Epiphanes but his influence is noted. Jesus visited Jerusalem for the Feast of Dedication in mid-December, an event now marked by the festival of Chanukah. Antiochus became ruler of the Seleucid kingdom in 175 BC at age 40.

He was the fourth Antiochus to rule the kingdom consisting of Syria, Cilicia along the northeast coast of the Mediterranean, land as far east as the Euphrates River, and Palestine. This was a former domain of Alexander the Great, which was partitioned by Alexander's generals upon his death.

For a third of his life this Antiochus had been a political hostage in Rome, a pretender who helped guarantee that a Seleucid treaty with Rome would be honoured. Released, he bided his time in Athens. He espoused Greek ways of thinking and action. Crowned at last, he proclaimed that all those over whom he ruled should become Greek in language, law and behaviour.

Antiochus established control over Palestine which was influenced by Egypt. He also sold the position of High Priest in Jerusalem to Jason, a *kohanim* (priest). Jason agreed to promote Greek influence throughout area. Jason was soon replaced by Menelaus who offered Antiochus a larger bribe.

Antiochus' army marched south intent on conquering Egypt. Rome ordered him to return north and home. As he returned Antiochus found Jews in rebellion against Menelaus. "His Magnificence" vented his anger by attacking the city on the Sabbath, murdering most of its men and taking its women and children captive. He left a strong garrison controlling Jerusalem, sacking the Temple and carrying away its treasures for himself.

Returning home Antiochus issued a fiat that throughout all his lands there should be but one religion, one law, one custom – all Greek. He ordered that an altar to Zeus be erected over the altar of burn offerings in the Temple in Jerusalem. For devout Jews this was the tipping point that led to all-out rebellion. Multitudes of them were murdered for failing to observe heathen religious customs. Gradually a guerrilla operation developed that finally resulted in victory and freedom under Maccabean leadership.

To be sure, Antiochus affronted all Jews by desecrating the Temple, both by sacrificing swine's flesh on it, and by introducing Greek practices of gymnasia to the sacred temple courts. He fuelled a private rebellion in the heart of every Jew. To match the audacity of Antiochus, came the Maccabee family to rouse the Jews militarily and spiritually.

THE MACCABEE FAMILY

The Maccabees are more properly called Hasmoneans. They provided military, religious and political leadership for Judea during the Second and First centuries BC during the oppression of generals who had divided up Alexander the Great's vast empire. The Syrian king Antiochus suppressed Judaism and fostered Hellenism. This became a burden too heavy for the Maccabee family. The result was this family's rise to prominence. Some Jews supported Hellenization; others vigorously opposed it.

Antiochus, Syrian king, built a pagan altar over the Temple altar in Jerusalem. On the 25th of the month of Kislev (about December) 167 BC, his priests made the first sacrifice to Zeus. The defiance and daring of an aged Mattathias Maccabee resulted in his five sons fleeing to the hills to coalesce zealot rebels opposing Antiochus. Judas was one of five sons. His surname, Maccabaeus, was the popular name given to the family and its followers.

Judas' guerilla war turned into full scale military engagements. Small Jewish armies defeated stronger Syrian armies. Judas' forces captured much of Jerusalem and rededicated the Temple, demolished the defiled altar and rebuilt it on 25 Kislev 164 BC. Festivities continuing for eight days. This Feast of Dedication (Chanukah) continues.

Judas Maccabaeus continued the war for independence. He was killed in battle. His brothers took over after his death. The last of Mattathias' five sons, Simon, gained recognition for Judean independence. Through him the Hasmonean house became a dynasty. Simon held hereditary titles of high priest, commander-in-chief, and ethnarch of the Jews.

THE HERODS

Antipater was Herod's grandfather. He became military commander of Palestina. Antipater was an Idumean. Their clan had been converted forcibly to Judaism by John Hyrcannus, a Maccabean.

Herod's father was also named Antipater, or Antipas. He was a skilled soldier, shrewd politician and diplomat. He and his wife Cypros had four sons and one daughter. The two eldest, Phasaelus and Herod, were respectively nominated by their father as Governors of Judea and Galilee.

In 40 BC, Herod was appointed King of the Jews by the Roman senate but not without political manoeuvres and likely by bribes. With the backing of Marc Antony, he succeeded in being posted to rule Jerusalem. Herod, totally loyal to Rome, was known for his grandiose and magnificent building programs. Historians describe him as a megalomaniac. He ruled with an iron fist for 33 years.

In honour of Augustus Caesar, Herod rebuilt Samaria into the city "Sebaste," the Greek word for Augustus. He built the city of Caesarea Maritima as a major port and Roman administrative centre for Palestine. Noteworthy in Caesarea Maritima are the blocks of stone with which the breakwater was constructed, sewers designed to be flushed into the sea, and theatres and temples. Herod's reconstruction of the Temple in Jerusalem was the crown of his construction efforts. Begun in 20 BC the project took 82 years to complete. This was the Temple which Jesus and his disciples knew. Romans destroyed it in AD 70.

For a while the Jews enjoyed a privileged peace in their homeland. They occupied the land of Galilee in the north of the former unified nation, as well as in Judah and the south. Between them were the Samaritans whose racial and spiritual qualifications seemed to be incompatible. They were both, Jews and Samaritans, soon to endure a new occupier of their lands.

The occupiers came to the land of the Jews and Samaritans by way of Herod and his relatives. Whatever negatives may be laid against Herod the Great, there is no question that this megalomaniac was responsible for building Jerusalem larger and more beautiful than anyone before him – or since. The Romans named Herod's mini-empire Palestina and considered it a province of Rome.

As a province, Palestina enjoyed a curious freedom in which Jewish merchants thrived and traded throughout the empire. When Herod renewed the Temple he courted the favour of the religious politicians. In the religious sphere, the simple synagogue and Torah-teaching reforms of Ezra 400 years earlier, became more complicated. The religious leaders were not monolithic. Indeed they vied with one another for the ears of the people. Often the groups engaged in legal entanglements. Beneath the religious differences were some significant spiritual purposes. Jesus, for example, applauded the "righteousness" of the Pharisees whose sincere zeal for observance of the law led to very strict regulations for all Jews in their quest for God.

The Pharisees helped with the development of synagogue worship, conducted schools and encouraged the reading of the Torah. They were very strict in their behaviour – sometimes even amusingly so. Accounts tell how they were so "religious" that they would tithe even the herbs in their kitchens. Lest they stray in the pursuit of godly

PHARISEES

Pharisees were associated with synagogues. Sadducees were associated with the Temple. The former numbered about 6,000 in Jesus' time and were right living, often legalistic about their halakah or walking with God.

The name "Pharisee" means the "separate ones." They were among reform groups that emerged during the Maccabean period in the second century BC. They emerged as reformers and in many ways were liberal. They promoted a strict observance of the Law of Moses.

The two groups were quite different. The Sadducees were part of the priestly aristocracy. They rejected oral additions to the written law. They denied a resurrection and thought God rewarded them in the present life. They dissed the existence of angels and spirits. In these things they were at odds with the Pharisees.

The Pharisees were in many ways closer to the teaching of Jesus than the Sadducees but they often argued with each other. Some of them were more open to the actions of the New Testament Church, except in the matter of Jesus' Messiahship or a claim to be the Son of God.

The Pharisee's hostility to Jesus was, perhaps, his popularity. He criticized them for their external observance of the law while they forgot its spirit. The Pharisees survived the destruction of the Jewish state by the Romans in AD 70.

Some Pharisees took time to study what Jesus said. Nicodemus was a secret admirer of Jesus, and is identified as a Pharisee. Paul was a proud Pharisee, but his participation in the group became first, his downfall, but ultimately his rejection of the legalism that often accompanied arguments put forward by the Pharisee party.

endeavours they were often known to close their eyes so not as to look upon a woman who was not their wife. Sometimes, walking with eyes closed to avoid seeing something they might consider evil, they would stumble, bump into walls, and then fall. Some of the populace enjoyed this sight and likely giggling, referred to these religious elites as "the bruised and bleeding rabbis."

Too often they have been caricatured as being insincere, when in fact, they were exceedingly sincere. As is the case in many situations, the reputation of a few spoiled the reputation of the many. Consequently the term "Phariseeism" has often come to mean hypocrisy, when in fact, the Pharisees were often warm, intelligent, caring, sincere religious leaders. The Pharisees numbered about 6,000.

The Sadducees were often at odds with them. Pharisees believed in such a teaching as a resurrection. Sadducees would have none of that. Sadducees were more centred in Jerusalem at the Temple, whereas the Pharisees permeated the Roman province of Palestina.

While the Pharisees and the Sadducees made up two of the main religious parties in the time of Jesus, another party associated itself with the family of Herod as having divine appointment.

The insecure Herod was always looking backwards over his shoulder to sense attack. He was brutal himself but nonetheless allied a number of supporters. Perhaps Herod's political friends had more reasons than conviction to urge the supremacy of Herod's family as legitimate leaders of the nation.

But as we shall note, the Herodians did not make for a popular movement. Someone described them as first century "toadies."

SADDUCEES

The Sadducees developed as a party from the second century BC to the first century AD. Their name means "righteous ones." None of their literature has survived probably because they were not writers but officiants. Sadducees did not believe in life after death.

They competed with Pharisees and other political and social groups. They were a weighty faction within Judaism. Many Sadducees were wealthy, as is attested by the excavations of the Great Mansion, with private access and private ritual baths to the Temple precincts. Sadducees were the priestly and aristocratic bureaucracy of Judaism. Many of them belonged to the upper ranks of the hierarchy, including members of the landed aristocracy.

They represented a strong conservative reaction to progressive religious views proposed by Pharisees. Sadducees maintained the freedom of individuals to shape their own destinies. Characteristically, they were very materialistic. They sat on the Sanhedrin council and generally supported the policies of the Romans to prevent conflict that could spoil their privileges.

They rejected the use of any other than the Torah in matters of law, favouring harsh punishments. They dismissed the resurrection of the dead, arguing that the soul dies with the body and that man has free will to determine his own fate during life. Their manners were considered boorish to the point of rudeness, even among themselves. They could be harsh and severe in the administration of justice. Yet they were practical and business-like in the operation of their nation.

THE HERODIANS

Herodians were cheerleaders for the rule of King Herod the Great, and subsequently his ongoing offspring's rule. It was also self-interest support.

Herod was a half-Jew. His mother, Cypros, had been an Arabian princess. His father was a powerful ruler appointed by the Roman occupiers.

Young Herod was a man of unusual powers. Appointed procurator of Judea by the Roman occupiers, he proved to be a formidable leader. He was physically strong, astute and had boundless energy. Herod was a master of political manoeuvre and extremely ambitious.

The Romans later appointed him King of the Jews, but this was not enough for Herod. He wanted coronation, not appointment to the throne. So after a three-year battle with Antigonus in which Herod was victorious, militarily speaking that is, Herod was finally able to crown himself King and Victor.

But he still did not have the support of the people of Judea. In his later years, probably as a result of having to force his authority on a people who hated him, Herod's rule degenerated into one of tyranny and brutality.

Ever unpopular with the people, Herod did not hesitate to act violently and indiscriminately to suppress any kind of trouble. The rule was always by force.

Most probably the Herodians were a group of people who favoured the House of Herod, a dynasty of sorts, and its right to rule over Judea. However, they wanted this rule to be under the overall rule and protection of the Romans.

Could it be that they were afraid of what would become of a powerful but unpopular ruling family if left to govern Judea free from Roman protection?

ESSENES

Essenes were a group unlike the more commercial Pharisees, Sadducees and Herodians. They came close to asceticism. They eschewed the excesses of worship experiences, thinking them to be contaminated by politicized priests who conducted the sacrifices. Both Sadducees and Pharisees helped initiate their earliest suggestions for reforms. That did not last.

Essenes lived mainly at the outer edge of villages and communities. One group settled at Qumran near the Dead Sea to avoid the Temple cult activities. This latter group wrote the documents we call "The Dead Sea Scrolls."

The Qumranites sought a just and holy leader, identified as "The Son of Righteousness." Recruits went through a long, rigorous initiation. Every day was crammed with long hours of study and hard manual labour. They ate meals in common. They dressed sparely. Most did not marry and may have been robed in white. There is some evidence that the highest order of the cult, dressed in white robes, were forbidden to marry. The Essenes believed their strict religious ways could hasten the coming of the Jewish Messiah and conclude this corrupt world.

Was John the Baptist an Essene? Did Jesus connect with the cult? Not likely. The teaching of the Essenes and of Jesus do not match. Both taught about a future. Essenes taught monks to hate their enemies, a direct denial of Jesus' words, "love your enemies."

Essenes later embraced militarism as a way to deal with evil: Jesus rejected violence. Essenes rejected the Jerusalem Temple and priesthood: Jesus lived in the world, not apart from it. He and his followers worshipped in the Temple and paid the Temple tax.

Some Essenes were married, some were celibate. A large community of them lived together in a region near the Dead Sea at Qumran. Most scholars opine that the Qumranite cult was basically Essene. Others lived in the small communities of Palestina, usually at the edge of villages. All were meticulous in their methodical and highly disciplined life of religious observances.

Essenes believed that all three of the other parties, the Pharisees, the Sadducees and the Herodians were corrupted by impure motives and behaviour. Ergo, they said, the sacrifices which were offered in the Temple were also corrupt. How could corrupt religious leaders offer valid sacrifices to God? The Essenes therefore ignored the entire sacrificial cult tradition, stayed away from the Temple and all it represented. They saw themselves as the spiritual people of Judah most interested in righteousness.

This, then, was the world into which was born, first John the Baptizer, and then Jesus of Nazareth. Rome, Greece, Persia, Babylon and Egypt had never seen the likes of Jesus – as we shall discover in our next chapter.

CHAPTER 11

ANNO DOMINI

Previously, in the last chapter we noted how the Herodian age dawned in the Roman province of Palestina. Herod, the local ruler of that province was the puppet of Rome. Yet, Herod was free to rule with his own style of leadership, namely a heavy hand. Evidence of Herod's insecurity is to be found in the fortified villas he constructed at several strategic sites, so he could withstand a revolt within his court. Herod murdered several members of his own family, including his wife, as he said, "out of very love for her." The slaying of the babies in Bethlehem after Jesus was born, was not out of character for Herod the Great.

JESUS, THE CHRIST

Many people have heard of Jesus ben Joseph but not all know who he was. The birth stories of the Bible tell us that Jesus was born to Mary and Joseph and lived in Nazareth. Because Mary and Joseph needed to register for a Roman census, the two travelled to Bethlehem where Mary birthed Jesus, a stable for his birthing room.

The Bible teaches that Joseph did not father Jesus but that Jesus was conceived by the direct action of God's Holy Spirit.

Because Jesus was *persona non grata* with King Herod the Great – the reason being that magi told Herod that a baby had been born who was king of the Jews – Joseph fled with his family for a while to the safety of Egypt as refugees. After Herod's death, the family returned to Nazareth. There Jesus grew to manhood.

When Jesus reached age 30, he was baptized and began his ministry of preaching, teaching and healing. At first, Jesus attracted many followers, some of whom became his disciples. But as his three-year ministry progressed, he drew increasing criticism from jealous religious authorities. Eventually he was accused of blasphemy, then treason, and was crucified. The crucifixion took place on "Good Friday," or God's Friday. By Sunday his disciples reported that his tomb was empty and soon he was seen by all of them.

Traditional beliefs about Jesus describe him as God's Son, Messiah (that is, God's Chosen and Anointed One), and Son of David (that is, God's fulfilment of a promise made to King David). Christians believe him to be more than a prophet, teacher and healer, indeed to be fully human while also being fully divine. Christians speak of the incarnation, or God's visible presence in human form.

We are "the visited planet." Jesus is also described as God's Word – the full communication of God's unconditional love which the Almighty wanted to convey to humankind.

Jesus means "Saviour." Christ means "Anointed of God." "Lord" means sovereign ruler, leader and divine one. Thus believers speak of, and pray through, "Jesus Christ, the Lord."

Jesus' work was foreshadowed by Joshua; both were in the discipline of saving people. Just as the soldier Joshua was saviour of his people and brought them into their promised land, the new Joshua – Jesus – would likewise save his people and bring them to a different kind of eternal promised land. Jesus' earthly ancestry was traced back to the early pioneers of Israelite faith. Some of them were giants; others had a less respected spiritual contribution to the faith process. One of them was Rahab.

RAHAB: JESUS' ANCESTRY

Jericho was a walled city for which entry could only be made through the gates. Its walls contained rooms and small apartments. Two spies sent by Joshua to scout the city's defences visited one of the wall dwellings domiciled by a harlot named Rahab. The spies were not interested in her business.

On seeking a place to hide from Jericho's leaders, they found Rahab. Obviously men entering her home would be watched and timed. Enquiries followed. When Jericho's authorities sought these visitors they saw entering the city, the neighbourhood wags were ready to tell about Rahab and their "visitors."

Rahab told the spies that it was well-known what the LORD God of Israel had done and was doing for his Israelite people. She hid both of them from the authorities and instructed Joshua and Caleb how to avoid detection. She sent them into the hills, west of Jericho, and told the authorities that they had left and now were headed east for the Jordan crossing. (Was this a moral lie?)

The spies Joshua and Caleb told Rahab that when the invasion came, she should lower a scarlet cord from her window along the wall as the Israelites approached. She and her family would then be spared.

Jericho collapsed, Rahab and her family were spared. But that is not the end of Rahab's story. In Matthew's gospel, the genealogy of Jesus records Rahab in the ancestry of Jesus. Later, Rahab married Salmon, a prince of the tribe of Judah.

In that line there would come forth David and in time past David, would be born the Messiah, Jesus.

Bethlehem's Church of the Nativity marks the traditional site of the inn where Mary and Joseph were refused accommodation. Beneath the existing building is a cave, which tradition says, marks the cave which was used as a stable – and here Jesus was born.

The Christmas story could not have been invented. It is far too beautiful to be created from human imagination. One gospel tells how a group of shepherds, their sheep safely kept within the fold – likely a nearby cave – received a heavenly visitation to alert them to the birth of a baby boy in Bethlehem. As the story goes, they said to each other, "Let us now go even unto Bethlehem and see this thing which has come to pass." They went immediately to Bethlehem and "found Mary, and Joseph – and the baby lying in the manger." Shepherds represented the poor and non-observant.

A second gospel relates how a star in the east guided magi from the east to find the baby Jesus. Who were these magi? They may have been Persian astrologers. Persians were strong advocates of the influence of the stars. They also may have been Nabateans, who lived in desert regions on both sides of the Great Rift Valley which connects the Red Sea to the Dead Sea. Magi represented the gentile rich.

Nabatean cities thrived for a time because of the spices which were toted from the port of Eilat through the Roman province of Palestina and across the Mediterranean to ports throughout the empire of Rome. Jewish merchants plied their trade even within the Temple precincts, buying and selling great quantities of the spices in Jerusalem at the Stoa or the Royal Basilica. Romans taxed the spices and dealers simply added to the price as they were passed along the trader chain. Such a tax collector was Levi, also called Matthew, who later became a disciple of Jesus and provided for us a record of his life – the Gospel of Matthew.

NABATEANS

Nabateans played a significant role in Palestinian political economy just prior to Jesus' birth.

Although probably Arabic by blood, they came to speak a dialect of Aramaic. The Nabatean bedouins settled in the Negev where they built desert cities: Petra, Avdat, and Shivta are three such cities. Former Edomite and Moabite towns were redeveloped as protective fortresses. These guarded their far flung camel routes – the principal source of their wealth.

They invented highly sophisticated water-gathering systems to support the population of these desert cities, especially in Petra. Their inventions allowed them to maximize the desert's resources.

Magnificent ruins of Nabatean temples have been found in Petra and in the Wadi Ram in Jordan. Artistically the Nabateans developed exquisite painted pottery.

Architecturally they used Greek and Roman classical styles. The treasury rock carving at Petra is remarkable for its scale and beauty. That they are found in the middle of the Edomite desert is impressive.

Eventually Nabatea was incorporated into the Roman province of Arabia. Nabatean culture continued to exist, particularly in desert agriculture. Petra suffered a series of earthquakes. It was forgotten by the civilized world until it was rediscovered in the 19 century. Since 1965 archaeologists have excavated the area.

Mary and Joseph and Jesus fled Bethlehem for a time, when warned of Herod's plot to kill the children of that town – lest there be a king of the Jews to replace him. Their escape route led them to Egypt, where as many Hebrew refugees before them, they found food and shelter. A Coptic Church in Cairo now stands adjacent to the location where tradition says the holy family dwelt in their exile. When the danger was over, they returned to their homeland, and settled in the village of Nazareth from which Mary and Joseph came.

It was the custom for all Jewish boys to accept their religious obligations at the time of puberty. Physical maturing also called for spiritual responsibility. From the teen years on, every male was expected to keep all the duties which accompanied adulthood. Ceremonies marked the transition into maturity. Such a ceremony as is now called a bar mitzvah.

Perhaps Jesus became a bar mitzvah – a son of the commandments. It was formalized officially as a tradition centuries after Jesus. No one really knows what happened during the "silent" years between Jesus' acceptance of his spiritual responsibilities and his formal entry into ministry.

JOHN THE BAPTIST

Luke records that Jesus grew, "in wisdom and stature and in favour with God and man." Certainly his neighbours were surprised at his accumulation of wisdom and insight – and they discounted him for it. Jesus' response? "A prophet is never honoured where he grows up nor among the people who knew him as a child!"

When he was 30 years of age, Jesus ventured south to the Jordan valley where John the Baptist had been preaching and baptizing. John was born to Zachariah, a priest, and Zachariah's wife Elizabeth was kinsfolk to Mary. John and Jesus were born six months apart.

WHAT IS A BAR MITZVAH?

When a young Jewish boy reaches the age of 13 he becomes bar mitzvah. Bar Mitzvah means, quite literally, a son of the commandments. At this time the young man is invited to join the minyan, a quorum of ten adult males required for the conduct of a rabbinical examination and public service in a synagogue. Thirteen is the age of responsibility. These teens assume responsibilities of observing the ethical and ritual teachings of their religion, as demanded by Jewish law. This includes praying regularly, fasting when required, keeping the Sabbath and obeying all ten commandments.

Is this the tradition that Jesus observed when brought to Jerusalem by his parents? Jesus went through all the conditions. He was examined by teachers, responsive to their questions. A Jew of 13 is well-versed in his religious teachings and ready to serve as a worship leader. His faith needs augmentation by prescribed rituals. He must now do good works which, when studied and understood in the light of God's commandments give content and meaning to a man's faith.

Until he is 13, no boy is required to observe fully the strict Jewish laws. During that period his father accepts that responsibility. But once he is bar mitzvah-ed, the full weight of the religious law descends on his shoulders.

Although no special service is required for a bar mitzvah, many families like to celebrate with their friends with a special gathering in a synagogue. It is followed by a festive reception in a home, or hotel. During this, the boy who is now a bar mitzvah, is called forward to the Torah, the sacred scriptures. He is asked to read from these sacred scriptures – and attains adulthood.

John assumed the role of prophet and claimed to be a forerunner or announcer of the person who was being sent by God to save his people. John was a charismatic ascetic who dressed in strange clothing, and invited people to repent of their sins, to be immersed in the River Jordan, and to conform to God's life style.

Immersion was not unique to John the Baptist. Every Jew immersed regularly, as preparation for daily events, and especially in preparation for entry to the Temple precincts to make his sacrifice to God. Immersion was a symbol of cleansing and purification. It had become institutionalized within the daily faith practice of the people.

Jesus insisted on being baptized, even though John the Baptizer believed that he was unworthy to immerse God's special servant whom he called "the Lamb of God." But Jesus, wanting to initiate his ministry, be identified with common people, to model an example and to foretell his crucifixion and resurrection, used his baptism as his entrance and announcement into his three-year ministry.

JESUS COMMENCES HIS MINISTRY

Jesus was in the synagogue in Nazareth where his Mary and Joseph raised him, and in the synagogue's customary way, took his turn reading the scriptures. The reading for the day was a prescribed section of the prophet Isaiah. He read the assigned Torah and Isaiah portion, placed it back in the hands of the attendant for safekeeping in the ark and, seated once more, expounded on the teaching of what Isaiah meant. Luke records what he said: "The Spirit of the LORD is upon me, because he has anointed me to preach good news to the poor. He has sent me to proclaim freedom for the prisoners.

PURIFICATION RITUALS

The Hebrew Bible describes how people could contract impurity in a number of ways: birth, contact with a corpse, contact with certain dead animals, the involuntary flow of liquids from sexual organs, certain diseases or the eating of prohibited foods. While impure, a person was not to have contact with the Temple, or its religious practices. Moral impurity may or may not be seen as the underlying cause of physical impurity. Qumranites connected ritual bathing with moral confession. Normative Judaism did not do so automatically. Thus John's repentance baptism was a surprise to many, especially where it took place.

Moral imperfections represented an inner defilement, a rebellion against God. Events on Yom Kippur addressed much of this. Physical signs of impurity were seen as the symptoms of this moral or physical imperfection. Impurity was contagious and had to be atoned for. A complex system of purification rituals resulted. The process of purification was accomplished in several stages: a waiting period, bathing and washing one's clothes, a cleansing agent such as water, fire or blood, the offering of a sacrifice.

Ritual purity and impurity were important in the literature of the Dead Sea Scrolls. The Qumran sect adhered exactly to the standards of priestly purity. The monks strictly observed Torah's laws of purity. In Qumran, purification rites were only effective if they were the consequence of repentance flowing from a pure heart. The Pharisees had similar practices. Destruction of the Jerusalem Temple forced the giving up of all sacrificial rituals, argued Qumranites. However, laws of ritual purity were retained. The miqwhe (var. mikveh, ritual bath) became important.

JESUS THE HEALER

Jesus performed many of his gracious acts of healing in Capernaum. One identifiable healing was Peter's mother-in-law. Her recovery was immediate and she proceeded to carry out her hospitality requirements as a host.

Jesus wandered through the streets, as crowds gathered, ever eager to hear the disputes that would arise between Jesus and the religious officials. As he was talking the ruler of the synagogue pled with Jesus to hasten to his home because his daughter was near death.

Before Jesus reached that home, a woman with a gynaecological condition that had left her weak, helpless and moneyless from years of varied treatments, reached out to touch him, if only she might find healing. She struggled through the crowd and touched the hem of his garment. Jesus asked, "Who touched me?" This lady was knew she was healed.

Outside the synagogue ruler's house, professional wailers started their death rattling mantra. Jesus told the wailers that the child was only sleeping. He spoke in Aramaic,"Talitha cumi," "Little girl - arise!" in the little girl's ear. She recovered.

Galilee saw many healings over the span of Jesus ministry in that region.

and recovery of sight for the blind, release the oppressed, to proclaim the year of the LORD's favour."

Jesus returned the holy book to the attendant and sat down. "The eyes of everyone in the synagogue were fastened on him, and he began by saying to them, 'Today this scripture is fulfilled in your hearing.'"

Capernaum was the main city on the shores of the sea or lake of Galilee. Once in Capernaum, centre of his northern ministry, Jesus started to fulfil Isaiah's prophecies. Capernaum became headquarters for Jesus during his northern mission. Jesus tried to convey that God has a love affair with humanity.

For a while Jesus greatly impressed the crowds that followed him. Yet as we shall see in the next chapters, not everyone smiled as he walked by. In due time opposition grew against his easy style and uncomplicated teachings. The time loomed ahead when the hero from Galilee would become the common convict. He soon would be executed by the Romans, spurred on by a section of religious elite cheerleaders. Yet, Jesus continued preaching good news, then started performing what the Bible calls "mighty works."

Not far from Capernaum and overlooking the Sea of Galilee is the lovely Chapel of the Beatitudes. It venerates the place where Jesus instructed those who had come to hear the good news. The hill is a natural amphitheatre.

Over the centuries Jesus' teachings have impressed billions. Although many things he said had been previously stated, his authenticity, his manner of saying them possessed an integrity, a freshness and a clarity of style. Someone hearing him commented, "No one has ever spoken like this man. He speaks with authority and not as one of the scribes!"

Jesus was the master instructor. He used the surroundings – flowers, birds, eroded riverbeds, sowers and harvesters – to explain God's nature and God's purposes. His parables were all intended to show what God was like, what life lived under God's guidance should be like. He tried to

THE BEATITUDES

Jesus' well-known "Sermon on the Mount" is monumental in its simplicity and in its beauty.

"Congratulations to the poor in spirit, for theirs in the kingdom of heaven.

Congratulations to those who mourn, for they will be comforted.

Congratulations to the meek, for they will inherit the earth.

Congratulations to those who hunger and thirst for righteousness, for they will be filled.

Congratulations to the merciful, for they will be shown mercy.

Congratulations to the pure in heart, for they will see God.

Congratulations to the peacemakers, for they will be called the offspring and heirs of God.

Congratulations to those who are persecuted because of righteousness, for theirs is the kingdom of heaven.

Congratulations to you when people insult you, persecute you and falsely say all kinds of evil against you because of me.

Rejoice and be glad, because great is your reward in heaven, for in the same way they persecuted the prophets who were before you."

show ordinary faith, to simplify knowing God, to uncomplicate the average person's perception of what true religion should be like. He tried to remove the "fog index" from faith and make God's love crystal clear to all. Later, the once-cheered healer entered Jerusalem, marched to his death on a Roman cross set between the crosses of two thieves.

CHAPTER 12

CHRIST'S COMMUNITIES

Modern visitors to Israel and the occupied territories likely see more of that land than did Jesus. He travelled as far north as lower Lebanon and Mount Hermon. His eastern limits were the Golan Heights and the eastern rim of Lake Galilee, then the edge of Trans-Jordan. His visits south seemed to end at Bethany and Jerusalem, except for his birth in Bethlehem and that noted family flight into Egypt and return, probably along the Via Maris.

Except for his possible return to Palestina from that refuge along the Mediterranean coast, he seems to have missed most of the territory once controlled by the Philistines. He did travel through the central hills of Samaria – the Shephela – but likely not too often. The preferred route by Jews, in their north/south travels to and from Jerusalem, was by the east bank of the Jordan River, thus avoiding the "Samaria experience."

Probably Jesus attended the Jerusalem Temple more often than the Bible records show because it was the place where the LORD allowed his name to dwell. It attracted most male Jews three times yearly – at *Pesach* (Passover), *Shavuot* (Pentecost) and *Sukkoth* (Tabernacles).

Some of the Lord's neighbourhoods have enjoyed a privileged place in the hearts of believers. They include Bethlehem, where Jesus was born; Nazareth, where he was raised; Capernaum, where he headquartered for his Galilean ministry, Samaria, where Jesus confronted prejudice head on; Bethany, where the Lord retreated; and Jerusalem, where he suffered, died and rose from the grave.

BELITTLED BETHLEHEM

Going to Bethlehem is a mind trip. For most moderns it is an annual imaginary visit everyone likes to travel each December. The modern mind trip has a variety of diversions – the cultural aspect of eating turkey, mince pie, carolling and television specials – but the chief concern of Christians today still is to saunter along the Bethlehem road.

On it we meet Mary, imminent in childbirth; Joseph, the reluctant father figure; the mousey, slightly inhospitable innkeeper; the majestic magi coming from the east (Nabataean sheiks, perhaps?); and the night-weary, frazzled, awe-struck shepherds. Each was commanded – the innkeeper excepted – "Go to Bethlehem." In our mind's eye, most Christians travel there too.

Our perception of Bethlehem probably is warped. Today's Bethlehem is a fair-sized city. In no way does it reflect the community which existed when Jesus was born, probably four quaint farm hovels and a sleepy stopover hostelry. Even the carol, "O little town of Bethlehem" does injustice to the size of Bethlehem. It was not little; it was miniscule. Google mapping would omit it!

So small was the birthplace of Jesus that the Lord was always known as "Jesus of Nazareth," never "Jesus of Bethlehem." And, as we know, even Nazareth was tiny. Yet, the prophet foretold it: Isaiah described the little four corners in such a way as to hint that apart from the potential prestige of providing a prophet, Bethlehem was "the least of the little villages in Epaphra." Think small when your mind trips to Bethlehem.

Trouble is, you *can't* think small about Bethlehem. Giants stopped there. There was Samuel, for example, bent on choosing someone worthy to be called the king of Israel.

God sent him to Bethlehem. His road took him past Jerusalem to Bethlehem. God told him, as God did to Mary and Joseph,, as he did to the shepherds, as he did to the magi, and as he does to modern people, "Go to Bethlehem." Samuel went.

The scattered rural village elders trembled when so venerable, so noble, so well-known a man as Samuel came to their humble hamlet. "Is this a peaceful visit?" they asked, while quaking in their sandals. Indeed it was a peaceful visit but it was never a small one. Looking over the crop of tall handsome sons of Jesse, the prophet heard the theme from God that "little is much; much little." So the seer struggled with the voice of the LORD which said, "Pay no attention to tall and handsome . . . I do not judge as man judges. Man looks at the outward appearance but I look at the heart." So God, through Samuel, chose David as the anointed of the LORD. No small place, Bethlehem!

Wheat fields wave in the wind outside Bethlehem. This is to be expected. Bethlehem means "House of Bread." Its rural character suggests soils where wheat is sown, harvested, then ground into flour. Into such fields came a foreign immigrant widow woman named Ruth. By common law she was allowed to gather the wheat the harvesters missed and eke out her living. Hers was a burdensome task, picking a straw here, a straw there. Moreover, widows in the land had to make do, and foreigners were fortunate to have even such a servile system of providing for themselves.

Thus, in such humble fields a man named Boaz spotted the attractive young widow gleaning straws of wheat for her survival. Love flourished. Marriage followed. There ensued children, grandchildren, great grandchildren. In the grand scheme of things, Boaz became the great grandfather of King David. Bethlehem is no mean locality.

In the days when David became *persona non grata* with King Saul, the former keeper of Jesse's sheep developed a number of *ad hoc* brigand bands which either harassed the Philistines or protected David from the melancholia of Saul. One group of the "boys from Bethlehem" was a rag tag, Robin Hood-type known as the Adullam Gang.

Television writers would do well to read the adventures of the Adullam Army. Here is the stuff of which TV series are made. Desperadoes all, they were like the straw left behind in Ruth's story. David's brothers seemed also to be outlawed and joined him at the Cave of Adullam, the bandit's lair. Soon, many society cast-offs joined him (1 Samuel 22 *ff*). The Bible says that "people who were oppressed or in debt or dissatisfied, went to him, about 400 in all and he became their leader."

These nobodies from no place gave Bethlehem a bad name. Not only was the hamlet small, it was base. Where was Adullam's Cave? It may have been near Tekoa, about 10 miles or so east and south of Bethlehem, near the hills that rapidly descend to the Dead Sea. More likely, it was toward the Valley of Elah, near the place where David slew Goliath. Either way the cave provided a natural hiding place to harbour the likes of David and his pirates.

David held fond memories of belittled Bethlehem, mammoth memories. It is not hard to imagine how memories are evoked in a desert hideaway. Water! Whatever else people thought of Bethlehem, David remembered that the local well provided the coolest, wettest water of anywhere in his orbit. Alas the Philistines now occupied Bethlehem. The Bible records that "David got homesick." He was homesick for Bethlehem. If only David could go to Bethlehem!

There followed that incident one of the most glorious actions of devotion written in human history – how three of David's men, out of love for and loyalty to him, stealthily entered Bethlehem and drew water from the well. The three said to themselves, "We will go to Bethlehem." David, so moved by this act of courage and devotion, dared not drink the water but poured it out as a thankoffering to God. Was there ever a more loving present to God than the sweet water of Bethlehem's well?

Near one of the many sites of what some have considered the Cave of Adullam rest the remains of a more recent rogue related to Bethlehem. The Herodium is set on an artificial hill overlooking ancient Tekoa, birthplace of the prophet Amos. Herod the Great built this hill as a rest villa from his weary duties in Jerusalem, an escape location if needed, and as a final resting place for when he died. It was a significant fortress. Herod had heard rumours of plots against him, and he too heard the command, "Go to Bethlehem."

Few visitors venture to the Herodium out of reverence or respect for Herod. Rather, theirs is a curiosity to see the evidence that this ancient ageing megalomaniac feared even the infants of Bethlehem lest they provide a leader to usurp him.

The focus for today's Bethlehem visitors, whether by mind mission or tourist tour, is within the present city limits. A few, notably Jews, pause at Rachel's tomb. She died, as Genesis notes, en route from Bethel to Bethlehem while giving birth to Benjamin. The tomb is more than a memorial to Rachel; it is a symbol of many mothers who have died in childbirth and whose suffering and death has meant life for others.

A few more will visit the so-called "Shepherds' Fields" east of the present city centre. They may be somewhere near the city centre, but one must remember that sheep do not graze in fields of wheat. The farmers wouldn't countenance that! This likely is the area used by Ruth and Boaz. Caves dot the area and reflect the reality that many caves served as sheepfolds, the shepherd serving as the door.

Manger Square is the focus for many modern pilgrims. Christmas Eve witnesses myriad choirs from around the world who come to participate in a triumphal evening of praise to recall Jesus' birth. Choirs also heed the invitation, "Go to Bethlehem." Christmas is not only 25 December for some carollers. Westerners celebrate it then – too be sure. Orthodox Christians choose 06 January as their day to honour the Saviour's birth and Armenian believers opt for 19 January.

These three traditions share the Church of the Nativity, built directly over a cave, which by tradition, served as a stable for a local inn. Each tradition, Roman, Orthodox and Armenian has a separate chapel for its use. The original Church of the Nativity was built in AD 326, destroyed and rebuilt two centuries later. The mosaics on the floor uncovered in the middle of the 20th century, are said to predate the Persian invasion of Palestine in AD 614. Tradition says that the Persian invaders, awed by the mosaics depicting magi following the star, spared the Church of the Nativity from the intensity of destructions the Persians carried out elsewhere.

In stating that the Church of the Nativity is built over a cave, it is important to note that several caves are under the arms of this church building. One cave was once inhabited by St. Jerome, a denizen of a Bethlehem cave while he translated the Greek and Hebrew documents into

Latin. A subsequent version is called the Vulgate because it could be read by the common people. His name was officially Eusebius Hieronimus Sophronius. He was a contemporary of Augustine of Hippo. As a linguist, Jerome mastered the languages in which the manuscripts of the Bible were written.

A wealthy woman named Paula, sometime about AD 325, financed and then assisted in his translation work. He spent some 34 years in Bethlehem and died there in AD 420.

On the south side of the Church of the Nativity are other caves. A priest may try to persuade tourists that one part of the cave holds the remains of children who were slaughtered on Herod's orders when Jesus was born. Another portion of the cave holds bones of monks and ascetics who either were murdered for their faith by invaders, or who died in service of the Lord as faithful priests.

The main cave of the Church of the Nativity is the one below the chancel and altar, where by tradition, Jesus was born. Pilgrims come and go with regularity. They sing traditional carols, whether they visit in summer or winter, autumn or spring when the shepherds likely watched their lambing flocks by night. They sing in all the languages of earth: in Japanese; Korean; Russian; French; Spanish; Portuguese; German, Ukrainian; English – just name it! They sing for one reason. God gave his universal order for mankind to greet the Saviour, David's Son, the Word made flesh. "Go to Bethlehem."

NEGLECTED NAZARETH

Nazareth nestles in the hills of lower Galilee. Although it was nested there, it was also neglected. It was tucked away from Palestine's "more important" communities. Neglected?

Perhaps! By the elite, for sure! Yet God did not neglect Nazareth. Moreover, good things came from Nazareth! Prejudice sometimes contradicted this mood as it did with the disciple Nathaniel, who wryly asked, "Can anything good come from Nazareth?"

Nathaniel was a Jew from nearby Cana. Was Nathaniel biased because it was more or less controlled from the pagan Galilean centre of Sepphoris?

Sepphoris is Mary's traditional birthplace. Years after Jesus, Sepphoris became a centre of Talmudic scholarship. Sepphoris looked on Nazareth as a satellite. Like Sepphoris, Cana was not much further away. Yet it is hard for residents who have selected one community as ideal for living to hold a high opinion of a nearby district. A resident of Cana could hardly give place to a resident of Nazareth, could he?

Give Nazareth credit for some good – some great – things. A lovely young woman lived in Nazareth. She was unfazed by bigness. So virtuous was Mary in character, in spiritual depth, in obedient to God's purposes, that the Almighty chose her to mother his Messiah. Her integrity was such that she still models submission to the will of God. She was humble but had self-esteem. She praised God through her witness "All people will call me happy because of the great things the Mighty God has done for me."

A compassionate father lived in Nazareth. He held high principles. Joseph modelled understanding and showed trust and love in the presence of a perplexing problem. He loved Mary so much that he tried to find a way to save her from public exposure as an unmarried mother. We know little of him from later descriptions in the Bible but we know how Joseph cared for her, brought her and her child to Egypt and at the appropriate time, brought them both back safely to Nazareth.

Jesus also "came from" Nazareth, as Nathaniel put it. He spent close to 30 years in that hamlet. Here he was schooled, made friends, learned the scriptures and probably apprenticed. Neither the size of the schoolhouse nor the credentials of the teachers were factors in retarding the development of Jesus "of Nazareth."

The larger Galilean community of sophisticated Sepphoris watched Jesus mature in a fourfold natural growth – "in wisdom and in stature and in favour of God and man." Is that not a well-rounded aim? Surely the aim of all maturing youth should be to similarly seek goals of wisdom, spirituality, physicality and socially-accepted behaviour!

Some years later we learn that there was little faith to be found in Nazareth. Jesus could do no mighty works there. Nathaniel's generalization about Nazareth belies the fact that even in a community as secular, as faith-depleted as Nazareth seemed to be, it harboured a climate of high spirituality in a few – so lofty a degree of it, that God centred his plans on Mary, Joseph and the child born to them. He would be Messiah. God seems to use faithful people, even amid such stark secularism or pagan practises, to fine-tune his divine intentions.

COMMERCIAL CAPERNAUM

Jesus chose Capernaum as the centre of his Galilean ministry. Capernaum is the Latin name of Kfar Nahum, the village of Nahum. That suggests the Old Testament prophet came from there. Nahum is described as an Eshkonite, and Eshkos was located somewhere in the Galilee.

If so, it is good to remember that Nahum's mission, like Jonah's, was among gentiles. Jesus identified his own ministry as to Jews, Samaritans and gentiles alike.

In Jesus' time, Capernaum was a busy port and international traffic centre spreading along the north shore of inland Lake Galilee.

Because it was a crossroads for spice caravans and ships alike, it was more commercial that other centres in the north, more gentile than other centres and encompassed more non-observant Jews than most other towns. Levi, also called Matthew the disciple, was a non-kosher Jew involved in the hated tax business. Even the main synagogue was a gift from gentile to the Jewish community in which he lived.

Jesus had an identifiable residence in Capernaum. Matthew, from Capernaum himself, describes his community as Jesus' "home town." Once, when people learned he was at home, they came to the front door and invited themselves in.

According to Mark's gospel, when friends brought a paralytic man and his stretcher bearers could not enter the front door, they removed part of the roof of Jesus' residence and lowered the sick man into his presence.

Jesus' first response to the sick man's needs was to assure him of God's forgiveness. His second response was to heal the man and, with his caring companions, send him back to where he came from.

Jesus used Capernaum as his base for visits to other areas of Galilee and beyond. Despite its secular bias, Capernaum became his most viable venue for his teaching and healing ministry centring on the kingdom of God. Residents appeared to welcome him as one of their neighbours. Jesus launched his final ministry as he left his Galilean headquarters to face the cross in Jerusalem.

SEGREGATED SAMARIA

Most travellers between Galilee chose the route avoiding Samaria. In Jesus' time, Samaria was a regional area. In Israel's chronology, it had been the capital city of the northern kingdom, Israel. Samaritans were an interracial amalgam of remnants from the former northern kingdom, once transported to Assyria in 721 BC. When they slowly returned, the Jews, who had in their absence inhabited the land, resented these intermarried Israelites. The book of Nehemiah relates that toxic flavour.

The flavour remained tart in Jesus' time. This is evident in the Johannine account of the woman at the Sychar well. The ethnic bias is also reflected in the stories told about and also by Jesus. Jesus noted that one of the 10 lepers he healed was a Samaritan. Jesus' parable about how to "neighbour" became a lesson of how a Samaritan cared for an injured man, whereas the Jewish religious elite passed by the traumatized victim for their own reasons. Luke records that when Jesus travelled through Samaria no one would provide hospitality for him. He couldn't rent a room! The incident led to one of Jesus' cryptic sayings, "Foxes have holes and birds of the air have nests but the Son of Man has no place to lay his head."

The incident at Sychar, where Jacob's well is situated, is especially instructive. First, Jesus had to send his disciples a long distance away for food: likely no Samaritan would sell it to them. Secondly, Jesus spoke to a woman – a Samaritan woman at that. That was beyond unusual. Then he engaged her in a conversation until she responded to his good-natured teasing with a healthy interchange. Jesus opened the situation for personal evangelism until she believed and became a spokesperson for his messiahship.

BLESSED BETHANY

Jesus found Bethany to be a blessed retreat. Bethany means
"house of the poor." Its name reflects Jesus' love affair with
the poor. Bethany contained many homes built into its
limestone caves which dot the area. Such homes still exist in
Bethany. Caves were optional tombs, so only the poor would
choose caves onto which they could add a house front.

Today's visitors to Bethany may be shown a cave
dubbed "Lazarus' Tomb." The authenticity of the tomb is
very much suspect. Yet the cave itself offers a sense of how
bodies were disposed of in biblical times. Moreover, the
cave provides a mental image of the event in which Jesus
raised his friend Lazarus from death.

Jesus' affection of Bethany stems from the welcome
home he must often have entered to refresh from his
wearying work. Bethany was Jesus' place to "put his sandals
up," so to speak. The village rested on the eastern slopes of
Olivet, two miles from Jerusalem. Jesus' obvious sense of
retreat at Bethany suggests multiple visits there.

The Bible tells of two sisters and a brother – Mary,
Martha and Lazarus – who lived in Bethany. Mary, from the
Hebrew *mara,* means "bitter.*" Martha* means, "lady."

Lazarus, means "without help." The Bible reveals how attached the three were to Jesus and he to them. Were they among the poor, or were they wealthy enough to provide hospitality for visitors who often came to their door?

John's gospel identified Mary as pouring an expensive nard ointment over the feet of Jesus and wiped them dry with her hair. Mark's gospel identifies the event taking place at the home of Simon who had been a leper.

Lepers also lived in caves; indeed, whether rich or poor, they were relegated there by society. The story's location seems to provide cause for Judas Iscariot to react. "Why this waste? This ointment could have been sold for 300 denarii and the money given to the poor"

Two significant events took place in Bethany. One, described in the fourth gospel, was Lazarus' death and resurrection, giving Jesus opportunity to declare, "I am the resurrection and the life . . . everyone who lives and believes in me will never die." Luke describes the other event as a meal which Jesus attended in the home of Mary, Martha and Lazarus. It was a teaching and learning opportunity.

Mary joined the men sitting at the feet of Rabbi Jesus. That act broke a tacit tradition in which women were deemed unworthy to study with a rabbi. Martha, in addition to needing kitchen help, blushed at this social faux pas. She made excuses to get Mary out of the rabbi's hair!

She delicately asked Jesus to dismiss Mary from his presence and to help Martha in her required hospitality duties. Jesus saw through the obvious impropriety. He declared that Mary rightly should be his pupil and that learning about God trumped social nicities and table preparation.

ZION'S SLUMS

All eyes in Jerusalem turned to admire its dazzling architecture, particularly focussing on the Temple Mount. Tourists would never stop by the seedier parts of the city nor would they acknowledge such places existed.

To the southwest of the Temple Mount, just a bit over the hill, lay the Valley of Hinnom. Abraham, with Isaac in tow to be the sacrifice, once came to this place. However, Isaac's sacrifice did not take place because a ram became his substitute. In this valley, pagan devotees once offered child sacrifices to appease the god Molloch.

Fast forward to Jesus' time. Hinnom was a combination of city garbage dump (where do you put the trash?) and residence of society's dregs and outcasts, the very poor, beggars, the indebted, the lepers, the blind, the wounded, the mentally distraught and the forgotten. Fires burned all the day and through the night.

When Jesus spoke about hell and destruction, his illustration was set in this valley. Hinnom became Gehenna. Gehennah was the word for hell. "You brood of vipers! How will you escape being condemned to hell" (Mt 23:33)? "Anyone who says, "'You fool!' will be in danger of the fires of hell" (Matthew 5:22).

JEWELLED JERUSALEM

Jerusalem the Golden, is a fitting title for bejewelled Jerusalem. When the early or late sun hit the stones of the Temple and the Temple Mount, they radiated gold. Meir Ben-Dov, principal archaeologist at Mount Moriah's south Temple entrance in 1968 when serious digging began, in his book *In The Shadow of the Temple*, wrote of the magnificence of the Temple Mount. "It resembles a precious stone ring crafted by a master jeweller. The final product of a true artist will be a beautiful ring, not a precious stone but a precious-stone ring. This was the great achievement of the Temple Mount's architect: creating the setting of retaining walls and dividing walls with the precious stone – the Temple – crowning them all."

That was "Herod's Temple." It was a grandiose enlargement and retrofit of the "Second" Temple which was built during the time of Ezra and Nehemiah, some 500 years before Christ. Herod's ambition was to out-Rome Rome. His master plan included a spectacular capital city of Israel/ Judah which reflected all the splendour of Rome yet tempered with a Jewish ambience.

So great was the Temple area that once when the disciples arrived with Jesus, they gawked at its overpowering magnificence. The great supporting unbroken blocks of stone were as long as 40 feet, weighing hundreds of tons. Mark (13) records the disciples' reaction: "Look! Teacher! What massive stones! What magnificent buildings!" Jesus was less awed for he foresaw the day when the Temple would be no more. He was more impressed by the remarkable gift of a penurious widow whose offering exceeded her ability to give (Mark 12). True greatness, Jesus reminded his disciples, is the spectacle of a widow placing all she possessed in the receptacles for the Temple treasury – and the disciples were blinded from seeing that by looking distractedly at stones.

Jerusalem sported a hippodrome to provided a diversion for Romans addicted to horse and chariot racing. To the northwest of the Temple, a large Roman headquarters for army personnel – the Antonia – overlooked Temple enclosures. Its symbols of Roman deities offended the Jews, especially since it almost abutted the Temple. On the western side of the city, inside its walls, lay the palace of Herod, which in Jesus' earthly ministry, became a temporary residence for Herod Antipas. This dignitary was the Jewish governor of Galilee and Perea. Herod may have also used the residence to attend the religious festivals.

Apart from the Great Temple, the Temple Mount included a massive stoa. Its purpose served the populace for social mixing but it provided more. International merchants gathered here to conduct business in a social setting. They bought and sold caravan and ship cargoes of spices and wide-ranging merchandise. Some have speculated that more business was conducted in the freedom of this stoa than in any business centre of Rome.

Business of a different sort became commonplace immediately below the western edges of the Temple Mount. This commerce included hawkers of devotional needs, such as animals and birds for a suppliant's sacrifice. Jesus conducted his public rage against some of these same vendors, especially those who made an undue profit from changing Caesar's coins into kosher coins congruous with a Temple-approved offering.

Also below the Temple Mount, east of the hawkers' bartering, from the south pilgrims gathered to prepare themselves for worship atop the Temple Mount. First, the men [woman did this ritual elsewhere] immersed themselves in one the multiple *mikve'ot* (immersion vats). Immersion (*tevilah*) in these baptismal vats was essential to ritual purification, according to the Jewish religious law. This act conformed to *halakah*, the Jewish word for walking with God. The dozens of *mikve'ot* were filled with cisterns holding rainwater. This area of the southern approach to the Temple is called the Ophel.

Steps of irregular width became the stepping stones of pilgrims' processions reciting the psalter in as they gathered below to ascend from south to north into the Temple. The width of the steps may have reflected the meter of the psalms they recited. Then, after climbing the steps and immersing themselves ritually, the worshippers proceeded through the three doors built into the southern wall of the Mount, and climbed the inner staircase to the Temple area itself.

Between the pageantry of worship and the beautiful, bejewelled city, any visitor to Jerusalem could not leave unimpressed. Jesus' challenge was that, for man, the spectacle, pomp and architecture of the great city, had become more attractive than loving God. Thus Jesus wept over Jerusalem for its love of institutionalism and its neglect of responding to God's loving care.

CHAPTER 13

DAWN OF THE CHRISTIAN ERA

In the previous pages we watched how, in Nazareth, Jesus declared he would bring release to the imprisoned and enlightenment to the forgotten. By precept and illustration he simplified faith to those who wanted to know God. God can easily be found by any person with humility enough to call upon God in adoration. God, the great reconciler, is a Father who welcomes home vagrant sons, the great Lover of mankind, his creation.

At Lake Galilee Jesus invited followers to join him for his mission. He gathered disciples, a dozen in number, comprising some fishermen, a tax collector, an investment accountant, and a political zealot. Each of them left their income-generation to follow him.

Jesus shared his life with the crowds, healing and teaching them. On at least one occasion he fed them. Somewhere near this hillside overlooking the Sea of Galilee, Jesus accepted the small basket from a boy carrying five barley loaves and two Lake Galilee sardines, and blessed them. How the miracle happened we don't know. Did the boy's large heart create in others a sense of sharing generosity as well? It was reported that a crowd of 5,000 men, plus women and children were fed, and left enough for a dozen more baskets to be filled again.

Immediately following his transfiguration Jesus took his disciples apart from the crowds and asked them their decisions. They went to Caesarea Philippi, where Caesar was honoured as a god, and where devotees still travelled to worship the Greek god Pan. Pan's images were set in carved niches in the rock face.

THE TRANSFIGURATION

Accompanied by three of his disciples, Peter, James and John, Jesus travelled to a high mountain. Luke says the purpose was to pray. There Jesus was transfigured, transformed by a heavenly radiance. His countenance changed and his garments became intensely white.

Two biblical figures appeared, Moses (Law) and Elijah (Prophets), and talked with Jesus. These biblical figures are thought to have been translated into heaven. Elijah was expected to reappear as forerunner of Messiah.

Sites suggested are Mount Tabor, the traditionally accepted location. Mount Tabor is not very high and had a fortress on top. Perhaps Mount Hermon is a better suggestion. It is a few kilometres northeast of Caesarea Philippi and reaches a height of over 3,000 metres.

The Transfiguration links to Peter's confession at Caesarea Philippi. Other disciples had presented popular notions of who Jesus was. Peter said of Jesus, "You are the Christ, the Messiah." The Transfiguration came at a crucial point in Jesus' life. He was fortified by the event and the affirming voice from heaven, similar to his baptism, which said, "This is my beloved Son, listen to him." Jesus knew that messiahship involved suffering and death, a radical change from current ideas of Messiah's role.

Jesus' disciples were puzzled by unfolding events. The heavenly voice with its message was directed at them. His bewildered disciples later remembered the words!

Here Jesus asked the watershed question, "Who do people say that I am?"

They responded, "Some say you are Elijah, come back to life. Some say you are John the Baptist come back from the dead?" Some say you are "The Prophet."

Jesus asked then, "Who, then, do you say that I am?"

Peter blurted, "You are Messiah. Son of the Living God!"

"Yes, Peter," responded Jesus. "But you know that truth because my Father's Holy Spirit has given you that revelation . . . And Peter, upon *that* rock, I will build my church!"

Scripture records that from that moment, "Jesus set his face towards Jerusalem."

On the first day after Passover, friends of Jesus met his disciple band at the crown of the Mount of Olives, where the road leads from Bethany into the city of Jerusalem.

The friends met them with fronds and palm leaves, rejoicing at Jesus coming to the Holy city for the festival. Recalling the hope they had for Messiah, and remembering that Solomon once rode to his anointing on a mule, they sang out, praising God, and crying, "God save us. Blessed is he who comes in the name of the Lord. God save us, Son of David."

This triumphal entry was watched by friend, foe and seeker alike.

A few Greek visitors attending the festival found the disciple Philip, from the town of Bethsaida in Galilee, and asked to meet Jesus. Some religious elite saw this arrival as threatening. Others joined in the spontaneous Palm Sunday occasion's exuberance. It was a high point for a week that was down hill from there. Except that the next Sunday was the day of resurrection – Easter!

JESUS SETS HIS FACE TO ENTER JERUSALEM

Jesus took the disciples to Jerusalem for the week-long festival of Passover. Travelling southward through the east side of the Jordan Valley (to avoid Samaria) the group crossed the Jordan again to Jericho. This ancient city was once visited by Lot and Abraham, then an invading Israelite army led by Joshua, now by Jesus, Joshua's namesake.

Here lived Jesus' ancestor Rahab, the whore who had hidden the Israelite spies who were vanguards of Israel's invasion army about to seize the Promised Land. A blind man cried out for help – and Jesus healed him. A tax collector – a dwarf – climbed a sycamore tree to get a distant view. Jesus passed right under him, then invited himself to lunch with Zacchaeus.

Jesus and the 12 climbed the steep winding path that led by way of the Wadi Qelt into Jerusalem. Many a bandit waylaid his victims by this pathway.

They paused at Bethany – "the house of poverty" – where poor people lived in housing built into caves. Jesus visited with special friends – Mary, Martha and Lazarus whom he had raised from death. A banquet was held and Jesus feasted with his friends.

While they were eating, Mary arrived bearing an expensive jar of nard ointment, the perfume with which the dead were anointed. She wiped the perfume from Jesus' feet with her hair. Judas, the disciples' stingy investment treasurer, disliked that money was thus wasted.

"Better to give the money to the poor," he complained. "The poor will outlast me," Jesus told the household. "Mary has anointed my body for my death."

JESUS WEEPS OVER JERUSALEM

According Matthew, Mark and Luke, Jesus never entered Jerusalem after his early public ministry began. His final visit to Jerusalem was for the last Passover Feast which he was celebrate with his disciples. However, the incident of Jesus lamenting over Jerusalem suggests repeated visits to the city. What is recorded in the gospels only gives a sketch of Jesus' life and activity.

Jerusalem, the central city of ancient Israel, is at the edge of the Judean desert. Its perennial spring-like climate, is pleasant but its soil is depleted for agriculture. Jerusalem became a religious and political symbol of the unity of the people of God. Mount Moriah, or the Temple Mount, rises above the city of David. By extending the walls of the city Herod created an urban area of 32 acres.

The Romans conquered Jerusalem in 63 BC. Under Pompey, Jerusalem reached its pinnacle of grandeur and strength. This was a direct consequence of the appointment of Herod the Great as of Judea's king in 40 BC. Herod entered into extensive building programs. At the top of the western hill he built a huge palace complex for himself. His most spectacular building project was the Temple and the extension of the top level of the Temple Mount.

Tension between Jerusalem and Rome climaxed in AD 66. In AD 70, three Roman legions brought the city under Roman control. Romans destroyed it in August of that year. Israel's prophets had warned of the city's destruction, as did Jesus for investing in Roman security instead of faith in God. Jesus lamented over Jerusalem some 30 years before its destruction. He wept like that of a "mother hen caring for her chicks" – but few others saw the danger.

Jesus spent the next days ahead in various activities. He began in Jerusalem by attacking the money changers who overcharged for sacrifices which were bought for the Temple. He overthrew the tables of those who exchanged Roman coins for acceptable Temple coins. Coins bearing divine Caesar's face were not allowed in a Temple where God was worshipped. The Torah declared, *"You shall have no other gods before me."*

The money changers often scammed worshippers by overcharging the exchange rate. Jesus told them that the Temple did not exist to provide income for people; the Temple was a place of prayer for all people – including the Greeks from afar and the people from nearby.

Judas arrived with a guard. He betrayed Jesus with a kiss, and Jesus was taken away to the religious court, the Sanhedrin. It likely met at the residence of the high priest, now marked by Roman-built stairs which Jesus likely trod. The church of St. Peter of the Cock-Crow covers the site. Jesus may have been detained in a pit while awaiting his trial and its verdict.

Having been found guilty of blasphemy by the religious court's "investigation," Jesus was taken first to Pilate, this time on a charge of treason. Pilate immediately sent Jesus, because he was a Galilean, across the city to Herod Antipas who was in Jerusalem for the Passover. Herod, tetrarch of Galilee asked Jesus questions, ridiculed him and promptly returned him to Pilate, the procurator.

Again, the charge was treason. Had not Jesus said he was the king of the Jews? The biased crowd chanted, "We have no king but Caesar." Then it was "Crucify him." After that, "Release Barabbas!"

Jesus was condemned to die, flogged, and given his cross to carry to the place of crucifixion. This was his fourth

THE LAST SUPPER

During the remaining days Jesus visited various sites in Jerusalem, sometimes healing, sometimes teaching. Often times he was called upon to debate with the religious elitists who saw him as a threat to their prestige and authority and who read about God from a different, more limited page of the Torah than did Jesus. More and more the theme of Jesus' teaching stressed urgent matters.

Then the time came for the final Passover meal. The disciples met in a borrowed Upper Room, and prepared for the meal. First, Jesus washed the disciples' feet. None of them had thought to offer that service to him, so he offered it to them. Service is a key element of God's kingdom. God is prepared to serve us and we ought always be ready and privileged to serve each other, to serve any person in need. This is God's way, explained Jesus.

Here the bread was broken, wine shared, and a new interpretation given to the age-old feast of the Passover. Jesus told his disciples to be nourished by his broken body, to be a part of the New Covenant which God was making with his people through Jesus' broken body and shed blood.

With his disciples – except Judas – Jesus crossed the city of Jerusalem again and entered the Garden of Gethsemane at the base of the Mount of Olives in order to pray. Gethsemane means "oil press." Olives were gathered from trees at the crown of the hill, on the slopes and brought to a vat in the valley. Here they were crushed, the pulp discarded and the oil reclaimed for cooking, lighting and ointment for healing. This also symbolized the crushing defeat Jesus was about to endure.

THE MEANING OF THE CROSS: ATONEMENT

The Cross and Atonement are synonymous. The Hebrew word for atonement, kapper, means to cover, to conceal the offending object and so remove the obstacle for reconciliation. The psalmist spoke of "covering sin."

Atonement really is "at-one-ment," the act of bringing together the forgiven sinner and the holy God. Through sin, from Adam through today, the people of God make a covenant with death. Sin places a barrier between God and humankind. That barrier is removed by atonement.

In ancient pagan cultures, bloody sacrifices, often human, were made to gods as acts to appease them. Appeasement is a poor form of atonement. To atone for their sins Israel offered sacrifices of their "best," from whom they had alienated themselves. They sought forgiveness by sacrifice, through their priests, small animals whose blood was offered as atonement for the sins of the priest and the people.

Jesus, the priest, is mediator (bridge: pontifex maximus) between the people and God. The priest initiates the step of reconciling the people with God. God himself answers with the second step – forgiveness and absolution. Such atonement recovers the human / God covenantal relationship. The act of atonement cancels the covenant humans made with death through sin and restores the sinner to God's fellowship.

Jesus became purest high priest and purest sacrifice. He offered himself as a sacrifice for the sin of the world. The cross, the joining of priest and sacrifice into one act of atonement was sufficient for all time, and is God's greatest act of love and mercy.

and last crossing of Jerusalem. Down valley and up hill, Jesus brought his cross to the place of execution and there he died.

Jesus' story does not end with the cross. On Sunday, the "third day," as time was measured by Jews, Jesus was seen alive in Jerusalem and elsewhere.

Sadducees did not believe in resurrection. Pharisees did. Greeks had no place for such an idea in their many philosophies. There was a belief in resurrection in Egypt and it was prevalent 2,000 years before Jesus.

THE RESURRECTION OF JESUS

All the earthly life of Jesus pointed toward the climactic conclusion of his presence on the earth. His was a miraculous conception. His life work led to revelations about the heavenly Father who forgives sin and calls all humanity to heed his love and accept his mercy.

At first, Jesus' disciples believed his ministry ended with the cross – a terrible defeat for all he represented. Three days after his crucifixion, they discovered his empty tomb, talked with him and came to believe that he died in order to rise again. The cross pointed forward to the resurrection.

What evidence is there of Jesus' resurrection? None from archaeology. None from Roman history books. What we have is the testimony of those who saw his empty tomb, the grave clothes used to bind his body, and the eye witness accounts of those who met him after he was risen from death.

These included Mary Magdalene, each of the surviving 11 disciples, two believers who lived in Emmaus, just north of Jerusalem, and 500 others who claimed they saw and met with Jesus after he was risen from the tomb.

EGYPTIANS AND RESURRECTION

Egypt's pharaohs made every effort to make life last forever. They believed that the most important parts of their bodies were the body itself, their name and their spirit's "double" in their dwelling place. They believed in a resurrection but it contrasted darkly with Jesus' resurrection which was promised to all who trusted him for salvation. Egypt only preserved the Pharaoh. The pyramid is a perfect metaphor for Egyptian afterlife. The king is always on top.

Eventually, Egyptians developed an effective way to embalm a body as a fit vessel for the after life. As a first step the body was cleaned and then the internal organs were removed and carefully stored in separate containers. Surgeons removed the brain, pulling it out through the nostrils using an iron hook. Next, the entire body was dried by packing it in a naturally-occurring form of sodium carbonate. This drying duplicated the action of the hot sand but with less damage to the skin and in much less time.

The final step was to wrap the body in fine linen bandages treated with resins. The process of mummification took about 70 days and was accompanied at each stage by complex rituals.

In the burial chamber, servants piled stacks of food, drink, clothing, furniture and all other things the pharaohs would need for their new life in the next world. Included were small wooden dolls representing servants. In the next world these figures would magically come to life to work for boss.

A dead person's heart was weighed against past deeds. If he failed the test a deity in the form of a wild beast ate the heart and the person was lost forever. To help the dead pass through the underworld maps were supplied in the tomb.

These reports are each found in various places of what was called the Roman province of Palestina. The accounts are each found in the four Gospels of Matthew, Mark, Luke and John. Each tells the story of Jesus' resurrection in its own unique way.

The resurrection of Jesus has been a central belief of Christians since the event itself. It also has been the cornerstone of the basic Christian belief that because Jesus rose from the grave, so will all who put their trust and faith in his salvation.

The impact of the resurrection was enormous. The disciples who had always followed the directions of Jesus suddenly found themselves empowered and motivated to make their own decisions. However, they were not without divine leadership for they recognized the Spirit of God within their lives.

Emboldened by the resurrection event, and with a sense that God had not abandoned them but was indwelling them, they began to share their experiences and beliefs with everyone they met. They also felt led to take their good news to every corner of the known world.

For the moment, Christians did not see themselves other than Jews who merely believed in their Messiah, crucified and risen from the tomb. But as the numbers of believers increased among the gentiles, some Jewish Christians insisted that the gentiles first become Jews by conversion. That persuasion did not last very long. Soon Jesus' followers were on a different fork in the road of faith.

As we shall see in the next and concluding chapter, the resurrection of Jesus became the focus of a different kind of faith. It would have growing pains, yet dynamism for those who were persuaded to believe. Some Christians chose an inward contemplative, spiritual journey.

MISSIONARIES

Suddenly, the Jesus drama acted out on Palestine's miniature stage exploded outward to the extremities of the civilized world. A great missionary enterprise emerged from a handful of frightened followers, led by God's Holy Spirit.

The actors were untrained! But they had a great cast, a powerful plot and a ready audience. Overnight, as it were, they became an international force travelling to the borders of Rome's Empire and beyond. And as they travelled, this underwhelming band of unsophisticated missionaries recruited great numbers of converts from all races and social classes.

The burgeoning movement developed a double focus. In Jerusalem, Peter, John, and James "the brother of the Lord," led the main group of Jewish believers. New Testament records tell us these early Christians continued Temple worship .

Another Jew named Saul (aka Paul), was sent out by believers in Antioch to convert both Jews and Gentiles. This amazing man made several journeys which took him to Greece, Rome and most of the major centres of Asia Minor. He wanted to preach in Spain but was tried and put to death in Rome.

Early Christians told the story of Jesus, prayed together and shared in a special communal meal in which they celebrated Christ's resurrection from the dead.

From this pattern of gathering around the table on the first day of the week has come the patterns of worship we know today by many names, the Mass, the Eucharist, the Lord's Supper, Holy Communion. It was all to remember the life, death and resurrection of Jesus the Saviour.

> *Tradition tells us about the journeys of the other disciples or apostles. Mark went to Egypt, Thomas to India, perhaps to Japan, John and Philip to Turkey.*
>
> *Both Peter and Paul were martyred in Rome. Tradition says Peter, who had denied Jesus three times before his arrest, asked to be crucified upside down because he did not feel worthy to die in the same way as his Lord.*
>
> *Despite persecutions and hardships, the church continued to grow until it finally became the official religion of the Roman Empire under the rule of Constantine in the fourth century AD.*

Others opted for an outward journey of sharing their faith and service.

The once-frightened followers of Jesus were emboldened by the Holy Spirit which gave birth to the church at Pentecost, 50 days after Jesus' resurrection. Some 3,000 people came to faith that day and were immersed as believers in the crucified, risen and ascended Jesus, Saviour, Messiah (the Christ), son of God, and Lord. This Spirit experience positively charged the church to witness for Jesus throughout the Roman Empire.

Meanwhile Judaism needed to adapt to changing situations, for example, the challenge that Christians proposed believing that Jesus was the long-awaited Messiah. Another challenge was equally daunting – how to cope when Temple life, considered central to Jewish faith, was utterly destroyed by Roman conquerors.

CHAPTER 14

CHURCH ROOTS AND GROWTH

In the last chapter where we discussed the conclusion of Jesus' earthly ministry, we observed how the resurrection event invigorated Jesus' disciples. When the Spirit of God was given to the early followers of Jesus, they quickly spread the happy news about the gift of eternal life which God was prepared to give to any and all believers.

For the moment, Christians did not see themselves other than Jews who merely believed in their Messiah, crucified and risen from the tomb. But as the numbers of believers increased among the gentiles – the *goyim* – some Christians insisted that the gentiles first become proselyte Jews by conversion. That persuasion did not last very long. Others disagreed. Soon the followers of Jesus were on a different fork in the road of faith.

While followers of The Way, as they were called – that is disciples of Jesus – made their way into different areas of the Roman empire, the Jewish leaders continued to consolidate their own faith and practice. As we noted, a formal religious council met to regulate religious affairs of Jews. Generally, these were wise and devout people. Yet, as in any aspect of life, some leaders had personal agendas. This council, known as the Sanhedrin, was also threatened – not by the new branch of faith but by the imperialistic intentions of Rome.

After the destruction of Jerusalem in AD 70, the Sanhedrin sought both a home and a written codification of Jewish religious observances. It was obvious that if the Jews were to survive, during this Roman dispersion of Jewish

SANHEDRIN

Romans learned to use indigenous political structures to rule conquered peoples. In this way Rome created a form of indirect rule. Rome permitted local kings, courts, and councils to retain function in a semi-autonomous way. Things could go as before on a day-to-day basis, as long as final services and tributes were paid to Rome and the emperor.

In 67 BC Rome occupied Palestine. Romans permitted Jews to keep their religion, their king, and their ruling council known as the Sanhedrin.

The Sanhedrin was supreme in matters political, religious, and legal. It comprised of 72 members, including the presiding high priest.

The Sanhedrin was composed of three classes, elders, high priests and scribes. Some of them were Pharisees. They seem to have had life memberships. The Sanhedrin met, usually on the Temple Mount chambers in Jerusalem. They judged Jesus but should not have. He was from Galilee, not under their jurisdiction. However, the Council thought it had governance over all Jews no matter where they lived. As the supreme court of Jews, it handled both religious and secular matters. Rome allowed the Council a police force with authority to arrest Jewish citizens. It could not impose capital punishment.

The trial of Jesus, as recorded in the four gospels, presented problems for the Sanhedrin. First, he was a Galilean. Galilee was Herod's territory. Then his arrest after Sabbath began meant he had to be taken to the high priest's house for a preliminary hearing. The Temple Mount was closed by that time.

people, the oral traditions needed written unification. The idea was proposed by Rabbi Johanan ben Zukkai, who established a *Yeshiva*, a rabbinical school for the preparation for the written code. Previous rabbinical schools had been established, of course, some very famous. This *Yeshiva* was for a unique purpose, codifying the Law. It was established in Jamnia along the Mediterranean coast, south of Joppa. Later the Sanhedrin moved to Tiberias on the Sea of Galilee.

MISHNAH

In Judaism, much of the teaching on the law was kept in oral form,repeated from generation to generation through rote memorization. When formalized, this code of law was called Mishnah, meaning "to repeat."

The Mishnah forms the central part of Talmudic interpretation of Torah or the written law of Moses. It represents the thoughts of many rabbis. The move to provide a written record was largely due to Rabbi Johanan ben Zukkai who shortly before 70 AD sensed the imminent destruction of Jerusalem.

In response, he located a school to begin recording the Mishnah at the coastal town of Jaoneh (Jamnia).

However, most of the work of collecting and recording material for the Mishnah was done by Rabbi Judah Ha-Nasi around the year 200 AD.

The Mishnah was meant to protect or "build a fence around" the Torah, written law of what Christians now call the Old Testament. It did this by interpreting the rules so that they might be applied to the business of everyday life. Revisions continued well into the 12th century AD.

While the Jews struggled to maintain their people as observant and faithful, however dispersed and persecuted, Christians likewise suffered from the oppression of Rome. In spite of the persecutions, the Christian faith expanded. As one bishop later commented, "The church is an anvil that has worn out many a hammer."

Generally the Christian expansion followed the trade routes and highways which the Romans established. The first missionaries on these diverse communication routes were not the disciples, but believers from occupations of trade, or guild members, or merchantmen or soldiers. In spite of Roman intervention, Rome unwittingly provided the suitable channels of growth for the burgeoning Christian communities.

Some other Christians, sensed that their highest faith obedience was to separate themselves from worldly possessions. They fled to the deserts to live in caves. Others, being persecuted, found the desert regions a safer habitation. Still others found the quiet places conducive to spirituality.

Monasteries similar to St. Catherine's were initiated in the land of Jesus as well. Near Jericho, nestled high in the steep vertical hill overlooking Jericho, is the Quarantal, the monastery commemorating the temptations of Jesus. No longer a vigorous monastery, it houses but a handful of monks who maintain the place of devotion.

Not far from the Quarantal is St. George's monastery stuffed into a hillside, where monks established a place of meditation to recall the escape of Elijah from the vile Queen of Israel, Jezebel. A few monks maintain this monastery as well. High above the Kidron Valley, the remote desert monastery of Mar Saba seems to guard the rushing Kidron before it plummets toward the Dead Sea.

MAR SABA

The Brook Kidron flows out of Jerusalem, east passed the Garden of Gethsemane descending to the Dead Sea. About 20 kilometres south and east, it drops past the Greek Orthodox monastery known as Mar Saba. "Mar" means holy. "Saba" commemorates a fifth century monk named Saba, an early Christian ascetic.

The fortress-like monastery did not always look as it does today. For centuries brigands raided the humble residences of the monks and so in the 19th century, the Russian church with the Imperial Russian Government, built the kind of protection which would dissuade all but the keenest of bedouin pirates.

Commemorating St. Saba of Cappadocia, the devout leader of these monks who was credited with many miracles and with a life truly committed to God, the monastery attracted as many as 5,000 monks in its heyday. About a dozen monks live in the complex today. Their routine comprises practical chores, a bit of agricultural work, building maintenance, and the memorization of scriptures, as well as the prayer exercises which normally mark the distinctive monastery existence.

St. Saba lived in a cave nearby, as did many of the monks before the early chapels and rooms of the monastery were built.

Persecutions by the Persians in AD 614, and by the Saracens in AD 788, left many monks dead. Their skeletons, as well as the skeleton of Mar Saba himself, are on display in the 110-room monastery. The chapels contain many beautiful icons. Some floors are marble. Many religious paintings fill the rooms.

Visitors are welcome, males that is, and only ones who are properly dressed – no shorts! Women, who are deemed by the monks to be a distraction, may visit a special room only, a watchtower where they may regard the monastery from a suitable observation point. Even female animals are barred from the monastery which must mean no resident eggs for the monks' menu – unless imported.

In each of these aforementioned monasteries, the common threads are prayer and meditation, an ascetic life for the monks, and the copying of biblical scrolls. The scrolls are copies mostly scribed in the Greek language. Little did Alexander the Great know that when he insinuated Greek culture on the people he conquered, that the Greek language would be the means by which Christian teachings were propagated. Nor did the Jews of Alexander realize that the scriptures they translated from Hebrew into Greek, would become the scriptures used by Saint Paul in his impressive missionary service.

Christians needed God's prompting to recognize the universal nature of their good news. They were encouraged by the Almighty to cross cultural lines and to explain to everyone that God does not measure people by their complexion or their stature, their occupations or their status, nor by their habits and their traditions.

The idea of missionary service did not begin with Saint Paul, but with Abram. Abraham was commissioned by his God to be the father of nations who would become God's agent of divine blessing. As God stated to Abraham, *"All peoples on earth will be blessed through you."* The prophet Jonah, a reluctant missionary at best, was also a prophet sent by God from his Jewish homeland to the pagan city of Nineveh, a powerful city far north along the Tigris River.

SEPTUAGINT

The Bible is a "received" book, that is, it was provided by God through his several authors as if God himself wrote it. "Bible" means "library of books." Earliest copies were written in Hebrew. Then came the Greek revolution. Everything Hebrew was translated by Alexandrian scholars into Greek, including the scriptures. Paul's Bible was in Greek.

In Alexandria, Hebrew scholars pored over their manuscripts and came up with a Greek Bible (39 books plus apocrypha) so that people could easily read it. Seventy scholars no earlier than 250 BC, worked on the text,which became known as the "Septuagint" (from septuaginta = 70).

The Septuagint was a very disputed translation of the original Hebrew text and contained some disputed materials. In some cases bits and pieces were added to the collection and in other cases whole books. The order in which books appeared also changed.The Septuagint was the common translation in use at the time of Jesus, it came to be the form adopted by the early church. When Christians added their sacred books of the New Testament, the Church Fathers joined them to the Septuagint.

As time passed, Jewish scholars who had access to the original Hebrew texts rejected use of the Septuagint. At the time of the Protestant Reformation in the 16th century, reformers used their increased knowledge of Greek and Hebrew to reinvestigate which books qualified as ancient and undisputed parts of the Bible.

These Protestant scholars agreed to adopt the books of the Hebrew Bible as the correct shape of the Old Testament. Other writings were assigned a lesser value and titled "apocrypha."

JONAH

The book of Jonah is a written sermon in story form. It could be a parable, a way of telling a truth. Initially, Jonah refused to preach to the Ninevites. He was angry and resented God's directive to him; he wanted none of non-Jewish repentance and forgiveness. But the book's message is that in God's providence even a non-Israelite people might turn to God in repentance, worship and be loved by him.

Little is known of Jonah outside the book named after him, except a reference to him in II Kings, "Jonah, son of Amittai." The name Jonah means "dove"; Amittai means "truth." The II Kings reference centres around Jereboam II, one of the most illustrious and successful kings of Israel. The power which Assyria in his time exercised over Syria gave him the opportunity to extend his empire to rival Solomon's.

The Book of Jonah is about mission. Jesus used the story to describe his own death and resurrection, as Jonah, as it were, died and rose from death. Jesus foresaw a need for his death and resurrection to be told by missionaries, not just to Jews but to gentiles like the folk in Nineveh. The Lord commanded Jonah to go to Nineveh. For the Hebrews the city of Nineveh represented luxury and dissipation, unworthy of God's favour. Who would want Jews to love them?

Feeling negative about his assignment Jonah tried to escape. Instead he went to the seaport of Joppa (modern Jaffa). From Joppa found a ship headed for Tarshish in his attempt to evade God's command.

A violent storm frightened the crew. As a last resort, to appease their gods, the crew threw Jonah overboard. They felt the gods were displeased with his presence. God sent a great fish to swallow Jonah. He remained in the fish's belly for three days then was disgorged. Finally Jonah set out for Nineveh in obedience to God's command. Jonah's plea was that the people of Nineveh should repent of their sins and follow God's precepts. They did.

PETER'S STRANGE DREAM

Traditions are good but sometimes hindering. The Christian faith borrowed from the faith of Israel. Patterns long set, became prejudice and a block to real change. As someone said, the seven last words of the church are, "We never did it that way before."

With Jesus, God altered preconceptions of faith that mattered to him. He was inclusive, not exclusive and God expected his followers to be that way as well. Peter willingly shared his new faith – but first, only to people who looked like him, acted like him and worshipped like him.

Peter went to Joppa staying with a local tanner by the named Simon, and while taking his afternoon nap, had a strange dream. Cornelius also had a dream. He was a centurion stationed at Caesarea Maritima. He and his family, did not follow Roman religion but had a strong belief in God. His faith was active, known for his giving and caring for the needs of others. His vision led him to Peter in Joppa, at the home of Simon the Tanner.

In his vision Peter saw something like a large sheet that descended from heaven. It contained all kinds of four-footed animals, reptiles, and birds (kosher and otherwise). Famished Peter, heard a voice from heaven, "Get up, Peter, kill and eat." Poor Peter, as hungry as he was, was not about to break the kosher laws tied to his long-standing faith.

"I have never eaten anything impure or unclean," said Peter in his dream. The voice that Peter heard declared: "Do not call anything impure that God has made clean." The dream repeated three times; the vision ceased. Just then the visitors from the house of Cornelius arrived. They asked that Peter might accompany them to Caesarea.

Once Peter arrived at Cornelius' house he revealed his own vision. "It is not the custom of a Jew to enter a Gentile home [as he had done] but God has spoken to me about the matter of that which was pure or impure." What a change for Peter, who slowly concluded that Jesus' gospel was for all the world!

Throughout these chapters we have tried to illustrate the progressive nature of faith and its many revelations. God seemed to disclose himself in different ways to different people. Usually the revelations were made to individuals of special character. Sometimes the faithful advanced several steps forward only to slip back again. Many who were faithful were also fickle and floundered in their faith. Too often they were disobedient and flawed in character.

Yet God never gave up on them, constantly telling those who would listen that he was prepared to meet any who would come to him in trusting in the work of atonement by Jesus on the cross, and trusting that his resurrection would also be his gift to all who believed in him.

These chapters hardly scratch the surface in a study of the pilgrims' procession toward God. Faith, divine disclosure and hope is what satisfies the human spirit. It is a goodly procession which these pilgrims make, ever drawing closer to their God, always seeking in the here and now, struggling between "the already" and "the not yet." Yet in their seeking, the Maker allows them to find faith and continue their journey to the City of God.